HEALTH CARE ISSUES, COSTS AND ACCESS

STATES' ESTABLISHMENT OF HEALTH INSURANCE EXCHANGES

HEALTH CARE ISSUES, COSTS AND ACCESS

Additional books in this series can be found on Nova's website under the Series tab.

Additional E-books in this series can be found on Nova's website under the E-book tab.

HEALTH CARE ISSUES, COSTS AND ACCESS

STATES' ESTABLISHMENT OF HEALTH INSURANCE EXCHANGES

FREDRIK C. LEWIS
AND
ERIN O. WALKER
EDITORS

NOVINKA

New York

Library of Congress Cataloging-in-Publication Data

ISBN: 978-1-62808-575-4

Published by Nova Science Publishers, Inc. † New York

CONTENTS

PREFACE

A central provision of The Patient Protection and Affordable Care Act (PPACA) requires the establishment of exchanges in each state, online marketplaces through which eligible individuals and small business employers can compare and select health insurance coverage from participating health plans. Exchanges are to begin enrollment by October 1, 2013, with coverage to commence January 1, 2014. States have some flexibility with respect to exchanges by choosing to establish and operate an exchange themselves (i.e., state-based), or by ceding this authority to HHS (i.e., federally facilitated). States may also choose to enter into a partnership with HHS whereby HHS establishes the exchange and the state assists with operating various functions. According to HHS, 18 states will establish a state-based exchange, while 25 will have a federally facilitated exchange. Seven states will partner with HHS. This book examines the states' responsibilities for establishing exchanges, the actions selected states have taken, and the challenges they have encountered.

Chapter 1 – Report of the United States Government Accountability Office, on Health Insurance: Seven States' Actions to Establish Exchanges under the Patient Protection and Affordable Care Act, dated April 2013.

Chapter 2 – The Patient Protection and Affordable Care Act (ACA, P.L. 111-148, as amended) requires health insurance exchanges to be established in every state by January 1, 2014. ACA intends exchanges to be marketplaces where individuals and small businesses can "shop" for health insurance coverage. An exchange may be established by the state itself as a state-based exchange; otherwise, an exchange will be established by the Secretary of Health and Human Services (HHS) as either a partnership exchange, whereby a state partners with HHS to establish and administer an exchange, or as a federally facilitated exchange wholly operated and administered by HHS.

ACA provided an indefinite appropriation for HHS grants to states to support the planning and establishment of exchanges. For each fiscal year, the HHS Secretary is to determine the total amount that will be made available to each state for exchange grants. No grant may be awarded after January 1, 2015.

There are three different types of exchanges grants. First, planning grants were awarded to 49 states, the District of Columbia, and four territories. These grants of about $1 million each were intended to provide resources to states to help them plan their health insurance exchanges. Three states returned all or a portion of those funds. Second, there have been multiple rounds of exchange establishment grants. There are two levels of exchange establishment grants: level one establishment grants are awarded to states that have made some progress using their planning funds, and level two establishment grants are designed to provide funding to states that are farther along in the establishment of an exchange. Finally, HHS awarded seven early innovator grants to states (including one award to a consortium of New England states) to support the design and implementation of the information technology systems needed to operate the exchanges. Three states returned their early innovator grant funds.

To date, HHS has awarded a total of $3.8 billion to states and the District of Columbia (DC) in planning, establishment, and early innovator grants.

Chapter 3 – The fundamental purpose of a health insurance exchange is to provide a structured marketplace for the sale and purchase of health insurance. The authority and responsibilities of an exchange may vary, depending on statutory or other requirements for its establishment and structure. The Patient Protection and Affordable Care Act (ACA, P.L. 111-148, as amended) requires health insurance exchanges to be established in every state by January 1, 2014. ACA provides certain requirements for the establishment of exchanges, while leaving other choices to be made by the states.

Qualified individuals and small businesses will be able to purchase private health insurance through exchanges. Issuers selling health insurance plans through an exchange will have to follow certain rules, such as meeting the private market reform requirements in ACA. While the fundamental purpose of the exchanges will be to facilitate the offer and purchase of health insurance, nothing in the law prohibits qualified individuals, qualified employers, and insurance carriers from participating in the health insurance market outside of exchanges. Moreover, ACA explicitly states that enrollment in exchanges is voluntary and no individual may be compelled to enroll in exchange coverage.

Exchanges may be established either by the state itself as a "state exchange" or by the Secretary of Health and Human Services (HHS) as a "federally-facilitated exchange." A federally-facilitated exchange may be operated solely by the federal government, or it may be operated by the federal government in conjunction with the state, as a "partnership" exchange. All exchanges are required to carry out many of the same functions and adhere to many of the same standards, although there are important differences between the types of exchanges. States had to declare their intentions to establish their own exchange no later than December 14, 2012; to date, 17 states and D.C. have received conditional approval from HHS to operate a state exchange. States interested in pursuing a partnership exchange must declare their intentions no later than February 15, 2013.

ACA and regulations require exchanges to carry out a number of different functions. The primary functions relate to determining eligibility and enrolling individuals in appropriate plans, plan management, consumer assistance and accountability, and financial management. ACA gives various federal agencies, primarily HHS, responsibilities relating to the general operation of exchanges. Federal agencies are generally responsible for promulgating regulations, creating criteria and systems, and awarding grants to states to help them create and implement exchanges.

A state that is approved to operate its own exchange has a number of operational decisions to make, including decisions related to organizational structure (governmental agency or a nonprofit entity); types of exchanges (separate individual and Small Business Health Options Program (SHOP) exchanges, or a merged exchange); collaboration (a state may independently operate an exchange or enter into contracts with other states); service area (a state may establish one or more subsidiary exchanges in the state if each exchange serves a geographically distinct area and meets certain size requirements); contracted services (an exchange may contract with certain entities to carry out one or more responsibilities of the exchange); and governance (governing board and standards of conduct).

In general, health plans offered through exchanges will provide comprehensive coverage and meet all applicable private market reforms specified in ACA. Most exchange plans will provide coverage for "essential health benefits," at minimum; be subject to certain limits on cost-sharing, including out-of-pocket costs; and meet one of four levels of plan generosity based on actuarial value. To make exchange coverage more affordable, certain individuals will receive premium assistance in the form of federal tax credits.

Moreover, some recipients of premium credits may also receive subsidies toward cost-sharing expenses.

This report outlines the required minimum functions of exchanges, and explains how exchanges are expected to be established and administered under ACA. The coverage offered through exchanges is discussed, and the report concludes with a discussion of how exchanges will interact with selected other ACA provisions.

In: States' Establishment of Health Insurance … ISBN: 978-1-62808-575-4
Editors: F. C. Lewis and E. O. Walker

Chapter 1

HEALTH INSURANCE: SEVEN STATES' ACTIONS TO ESTABLISH EXCHANGES UNDER THE PATIENT PROTECTION AND AFFORDABLE CARE ACT*

United States Government Accountability Office

WHY GAO DID THIS STUDY

A central provision of PPACA requires the establishment of exchanges in each state—online marketplaces through which eligible individuals and small business employers can compare and select health insurance coverage from participating health plans. Exchanges are to begin enrollment by October 1, 2013, with coverage to commence January 1, 2014. States have some flexibility with respect to exchanges by choosing to establish and operate an exchange themselves (i.e., state-based), or by ceding this authority to HHS (i.e., federally facilitated). States may also choose to enter into a partnership with HHS whereby HHS establishes the exchange and the state assists with operating various functions. According to HHS, 18 states will establish a state-based exchange, while 26 will have a federally facilitated exchange. Seven states will partner with HHS.

* This is an edited, reformatted and augmented version of United States Government Accountability Office, Publication No. GAO-13-486, dated April 2013.

GAO was asked to report on (1) states' responsibilities for establishing exchanges, and (2) actions selected states have taken to establish exchanges and challenges they have encountered. To do this work, GAO reviewed PPACA provisions and HHS implementing regulations and guidance. GAO also conducted semistructured interviews with state officials in the District of Columbia, Iowa, Minnesota, Nevada, New York, Oregon, and Rhode Island. For this review, GAO refers to the District of Columbia as a state. GAO selected these states based on several criteria, such as a 3-year average of states' uninsured population and geographic dispersion. HHS and the seven states in our review provided technical comments on this report, which GAO incorporated as appropriate.

WHAT GAO FOUND

The Patient Protection and Affordable Care Act (PPACA) and the Department of Health and Human Services (HHS) regulations, supplemented by HHS guidance, require states and American Health Benefit Exchanges (exchanges) to carry out a number of key functions, for which state responsibilities vary by exchange type. A state that chooses to operate its exchange is responsible for: (1) establishing an operating and governance structure, (2) ensuring exchanges are capable of certifying qualified health plans and making them available to qualified individuals, (3) developing electronic, streamlined, and coordinated eligibility and enrollment systems, (4) conducting consumer outreach and assistance, and (5) ensuring the financial sustainability of the exchange. A state that partners with HHS may assist HHS with certain functions, such as making qualified health plan recommendations and conducting aspects of consumer outreach and assistance.

Despite some challenges, the seven selected states in GAO's review reported they have taken actions to create exchanges, which they expect will be ready for enrollment by the deadline of October 1, 2013. For example:

- Six states will operate as a state-based exchange, with most choosing this option as a way to maintain control of their insurance markets and better meet the needs of their state's residents. The seventh state—Iowa—will partner with HHS.
- All seven states have taken steps toward deciding which qualified health plans would be included in the exchange. Two states have decided that their exchanges will have the authority to actively select

which qualified health plans may participate in the exchange, while the remaining five states will allow all qualified health plans to participate in the exchange.

- All states are in various stages of developing an information technology (IT) infrastructure, including redesigning, upgrading, or replacing their outdated Medicaid and Children's Health Insurance Program eligibility and enrollment systems. Six states are also building the exchange IT infrastructure needed to integrate systems and allow consumers to navigate among health programs, but identified challenges with the complexity and magnitude of the IT projects, time constraints, and guidance for developing their systems.
- Six of the seven states included in our review are in various stages of developing a consumer outreach and assistance program to reach out to and help enroll potential consumers. As a partnership state, Iowa has not yet decided whether and to what extent it will assume responsibility for aspects of this function.
- Officials in the six state-based exchanges reported they are considering revenue options for financially sustaining their exchange. For example, three states plan to charge fees to insurance carriers participating in the exchange. However, some states reported challenges with developing these options, given uncertainties related to exchange enrollment, on which the fees are based.

ABBREVIATIONS

BHP	Basic Health Program
CBO	Congressional Budget Office
CCIIO	Center for Consumer Information and Insurance Oversight
CHIP	Children's Health Insurance Program
CMS	Centers for Medicare & Medicaid Services
EHB	essential health benefits
HCERA	Health Care Education and Reconciliation Act
HHS	U.S. Department of Health and Human Services
IT	information technology
PPACA	Patient Protection and Affordable Care Act
QHP	Qualified Health Plan
SNAP	Supplemental Nutrition Assistance Program
TANF	Temporary Assistance for Needy Families

April 30, 2013
The Honorable Charles E. Grassley
Ranking Member
Committee on the Judiciary
United States Senate

Dear Senator Grassley:

The Patient Protection and Affordable Care Act (PPACA),[1] signed into law on March 23, 2010, contains a number of provisions intended to reform aspects of the private health insurance market and expand the availability and affordability of coverage. A central provision of the law requires the establishment of American Health Benefit Exchanges (exchanges) in each state—online marketplaces through which eligible individuals and small business employers can compare and select health insurance coverage from among participating health plans.[2] Intended to provide seamless "no wrong door" access to coverage options, in general, exchanges will need to be able to determine whether individuals and small business employees[3] are eligible for a private health plan, Medicaid,[4] or the Children's Health Insurance Program (CHIP).[5],[6] This means that no matter how an individual submits an application or which program receives the application, there will be a process by which the individual can receive an eligibility determination using the same application, without the need to submit information to multiple programs. Exchanges are to begin enrollment by October 1, 2013, with coverage to commence January 1, 2014. The Congressional Budget Office has estimated that about 7 million individuals will be enrolled in exchanges in 2014, increasing to about 26 million by 2022.

While PPACA places some requirements on the design and function of exchanges, states also have a number of operational decisions to make. A state may establish the exchange itself (referred to as a state-based exchange), cede the responsibility entirely to the Department of Health and Human Services (HHS) (referred to as a federally facilitated exchange), or enter into a partnership with HHS (referred to as a partnership exchange).[7] Depending on the type of exchange, states are facing a number of critical policy and implementation decisions, subject to HHS regulation and approval. Such decisions involve determining individuals' eligibility and enrolling them in health insurance plans, conducting consumer outreach and assisting potential enrollees, ensuring qualified health plans are certified, and ensuring the exchange's longterm financial sustainability. In addition, states must develop information technology (IT) systems that securely facilitate the movement of information to provide enrollees with answers about their eligibility and enhance their ability to enroll in health insurance coverage. States are faced with unprecedented levels of data sharing and coordination between federal agencies, private health plans, state insurance commissioners, and state Medicaid agencies. As of March 27, 2013, the federal government has awarded states nearly $3.7 billion in grant funding to cover some of the states' planning and implementation costs.

You asked us to report on the actions states are taking to establish exchanges. This report addresses the following questions:

1. What are states' responsibilities for establishing exchanges?
2. What actions have selected states taken to establish exchanges and what challenges have they encountered?

To identify states' responsibilities for establishing exchanges, we reviewed selected PPACA provisions and HHS implementing regulations and guidance related to the following categories of responsibilities:[8]

- establishing a governance and operating structure;
- ensuring exchanges will be capable of certifying qualified health plans;
- simplifying and streamlining eligibility and enrollment systems;
- conducting consumer assistance and outreach; and
- ensuring financial sustainability of the exchange.

During our review, we obtained status updates on the development of regulations and guidance from the Center for Consumer Information and Insurance Oversight (CCIIO) within HHS's Centers for Medicare & Medicaid Services (CMS) that oversees the implementation of exchanges. We also met with CCIIO officials to discuss the ways in which they provided guidance to the states.

To identify the actions selected states have taken to establish exchanges and the challenges they encountered, we conducted semi-structured interviews with state exchange officials in the District of Columbia and six states: Iowa, Minnesota, Nevada, New York, Oregon, and Rhode Island. For the purposes of this report, we hereafter refer to the District of Columbia as a state. We selected these states on the basis of: (1) a 3- year average of the uninsured population within states; (2) the uninsured population in states in 2011; (3) the amount of federal exchange grants awarded to states on a per capita basis; (4) geographic dispersion, and (5) whether states will have a state-based, federally facilitated, or partnership exchange.[9] Six states in our review plan to establish and operate a state-based exchange, while one state—Iowa—opted for a partnership exchange. We also met with budget officials in some of these states to discuss the fiscal aspects of establishing exchanges, including how states will ensure financial sustainability for their exchange. The findings from these interviews cannot be generalized to all state exchange and budget offices. We obtained additional information from interviews with officials from state associations, including the National Association of Insurance Commissioners, the National Association of State Budget Officers, and the National Conference of State Legislatures. Two states that will have federally facilitated exchanges—Florida and Maine—were initially selected for inclusion in our review. However, exchange officials in those states declined to be interviewed. Therefore, this review focuses on states' responsibilities and actions related to state-based and partnership exchanges. A more detailed description of our objectives, scope, and methodology is included in appendix I.

We conducted our work from September 2011 to April 2013 in accordance with generally accepted government audit standards. Those standards require that we plan and perform the audit to obtain sufficient, appropriate evidence to provide a reasonable basis for our findings and conclusions based on our audit objectives. We believe that the evidence obtained provides a reasonable basis for our findings and conclusions based on our audit objectives.

BACKGROUND

Exchanges are online marketplaces where eligible individuals and small businesses can purchase health insurance. PPACA prescribes a seamless, streamlined eligibility process for consumers to submit a single application and receive an eligibility determination for enrollment in a qualified health plan through the exchange, advance payments of the premium tax credit,[10] cost sharing reductions,[11] Medicaid, CHIP, and the Basic Health Program (BHP),[12] if applicable.

Under PPACA, an exchange must be operational in each state by January 1, 2014. States have some flexibility with respect to exchanges, by choosing to establish and operate an exchange themselves (referred to as a state-based exchange) or by ceding this authority to HHS (referred to as a federally facilitated exchange).[13] States choosing to establish a state-based exchange were required to submit an application "blueprint" to HHS by December 14, 2012. Subject to HHS review and approval, the blueprint detailed how the states planned to implement various functions and activities that HHS deemed essential to operating this type of exchange. HHS identified a third type of exchange states could choose, referred to as a partnership exchange. According to HHS, a partnership exchange is a variation of a federally facilitated exchange, whereby HHS establishes and generally operates the exchange and the state assists HHS with operating various functions of the exchange. States opting for a partnership exchange were required to submit an application blueprint to HHS by February 15, 2013, detailing how the state planned to implement various functions and activities. According to HHS, as of March 14, 2013, 18 states have opted to establish a state-based exchange. In another 7 states, HHS will establish and operate a partnership exchange, with states assisting in certain functions (see figure 1). HHS's approval of these exchanges is conditional on the states' addressing a list of activities highlighted in the state's application blueprint. HHS will establish a federally facilitated exchange in the remaining 26 states.

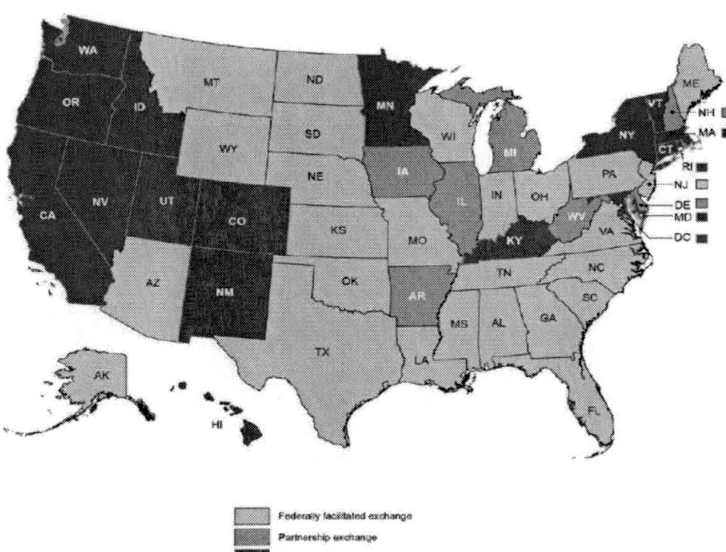

Source: GAO analysis of CMS data; Map Resources (map).

Figure 1. Distribution of State Decisions on Exchange Type, as of March 14, 2013.

Regardless of the type of exchange states plan to establish, open enrollment in the exchange is to begin on October 1, 2013. See figure 2 for a timeline of key milestones under PPACA.

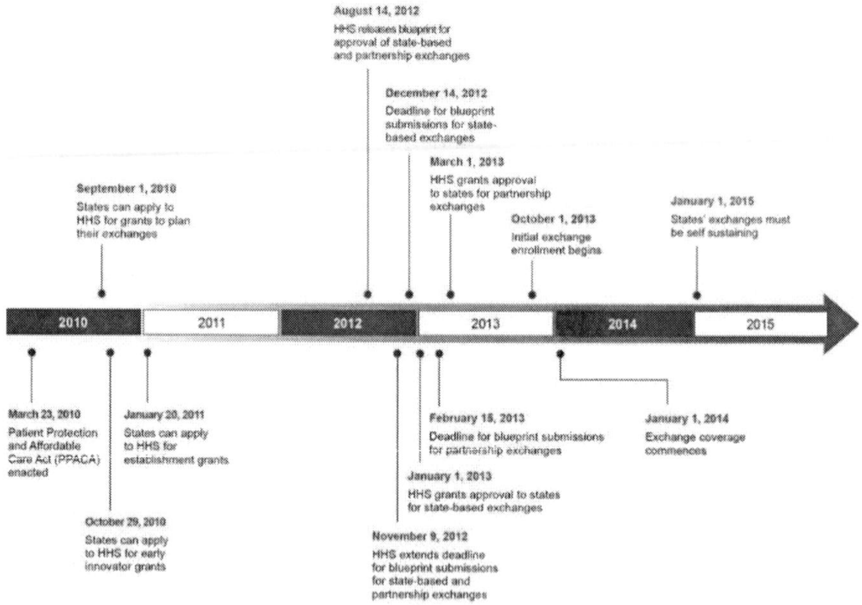

Source: GAO analysis of relevant PPACA provisions and HHS regulations and guidance.

Figure 2. Timeline for Key Exchange Milestones.

To help states establish an exchange, federal grants are available for planning and implementation activities, as well as for the first year of an exchange's operation. As shown in figure 2, beginning in September 2010, states could apply for up to $1 million in planning grants to conduct initial research and exchange planning activities.[14] Establishment grants became available to eligible states to set up their own exchanges or to support activities related to the establishment of partnership exchanges or federally facilitated exchanges in the state.[15] States could also apply for "early innovator" grants to help them develop and adapt technology systems to determine eligibility and enrollment. These grants were awarded in 2011 to states that demonstrated an ability to develop IT systems on a fast track schedule and a willingness to share design and implementation solutions with other states. Between September 2010 and March 2013, HHS awarded exchange grants totaling nearly \$3.7 billion to 50 states.[16,17] Of that amount, states returned over \$98 million in grant awards.[18] HHS awarded over \$1 billion dollars to the 7 states in our review—New York and Oregon were awarded the largest amounts. Figure 3 shows the range of exchange grant funding by state as of March 27, 2013.

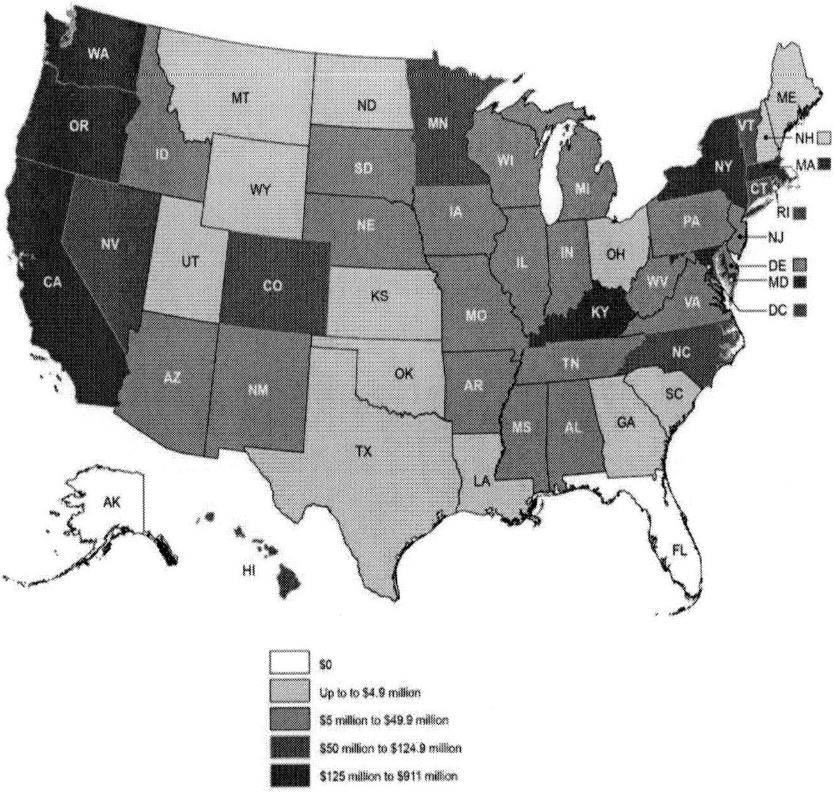

Source: GAO analysis of CMS data, Map Resources (Map).

[a]Grant funding reflects the total amounts awarded minus amounts that a state returned. As noted earlier, certain states have returned this funding to HHS for reasons such as a state's decision not to pursue a state-based exchange.

Figure 3. Range of exchange grant funding by state, as of March 27, 2013.[a]

States' Responsibilities for Establishing Exchanges Vary, Depending on the Type of Exchange

PPACA and HHS implementing regulations and guidance require states and exchanges to carry out a number of key functions, for which state responsibilities vary by exchange type. A state that chooses to run its own exchange is responsible for: establishing an operating and governance structure, ensuring QHPs are certified and available to qualified individuals,[19] streamlining eligibility and enrollment systems, conducting consumer outreach and assistance, and ensuring the financial sustainability of the exchange. A state that has created a partnership exchange may assist HHS in some of these functions, such as making QHP certification recommendations and conducting aspects of consumer outreach and assistance.

States Must Establish an Operating and Governance Structure

A state choosing to operate a state-based exchange must establish the operating and governance structure through which the exchange will be run and managed. Specifically, the state must determine whether the exchange will be run as a governmental agency or a nonprofit organization. Regardless of whether the exchange will be run as a governmental agency or a nonprofit, the state has the authority to allow an exchange to contract with other entities to carry out one or more responsibilities of the exchange.[20]

Further, a state operating an exchange as an independent state agency or nonprofit entity established by the state must establish a governance board that meets certain requirements. For example, the board must be administered under a publicly adopted operating charter or by-laws, ensure the board's membership includes at least one voting member who is a consumer representative and is not made up of a majority of voting representatives with conflicts of interest (for example, representatives of health insurance issuers), and ensure that a majority of the voting members have relevant health care experience (for example, health benefits administration or public health).

States Must Ensure Exchanges Will Be Capable of Certifying Qualified Health Plans

States choosing to operate their own exchange must ensure the exchange will be capable of certifying qualified health plans (QHP) and making them available to qualified individuals. A state opting for a partnership exchange may choose to engage in this function. In a partnership exchange, health insurance issuers will work directly with the state to submit all QHP issuer application information in accordance with state guidance.[21] An exchange may only offer health plans that are certified as a QHP. To be certified, a health plan must meet two categories of requirements: (1) the health insurance issuer must be in compliance with minimum certification requirements as defined by HHS; and (2) the availability of the health plan through an exchange must be in the interest of qualified individuals and employers. To meet the minimum certification requirements, health insurance issuers must, for example, (1) be licensed and in good standing in each state in which the insurance coverage is offered,[22] (2) comply with quality improvement standards, and (3) ensure their plan networks are adequate and include essential community health providers, where available, to provide timely access to services for predominantly low-income, medically underserved individuals.

How an exchange determines whether a plan is in the interest of qualified individuals and employers may depend on how the state organizes its market. The state may choose to organize its market as an "active purchaser" or as a "passive purchaser." As an active purchaser, the state will decide which health plans can be offered in the exchange on the basis of such factors as select criteria, quality, and price. As a passive purchaser, the state may permit all QHPs to participate in the exchange.

In order to be certified as a QHP, plans will also need to meet certain coverage requirements. Specifically, PPACA requires that QHPs provide essential health benefits (EHB) which include coverage within 10 categories:

1. Ambulatory patient services,
2. Emergency services,
3. Hospitalization,
4. Maternity and newborn care,
5. Mental health benefits and substance abuse disorder services, including behavioral health treatment,
6. Prescription drugs,
7. Rehabilitative and habilitative services and devices,

8. Laboratory services,
9. Preventive and wellness services and chronic disease management, and
10. Pediatric services including oral and vision care.[23]

In addition, within an exchange, health insurance issuers may offer QHPs at one of four levels of coverage that reflect out-of-pocket expenses for an enrollee. The four levels of coverage correspond to a percentage paid by a health plan of the total allowed costs of benefit designated by metal tiers: 60 percent (bronze), 70 percent (silver), 80 percent (gold), and 90 percent (platinum).[24] At a minimum, however, a health insurance issuer must offer QHPs at both the silver and gold levels of coverage.

States may choose to identify a benchmark plan for their state that, at a minimum, covers the EHB. According to HHS, the benchmark plan reflects the scope of services and limits offered by a "typical employer" plan in the state.[25] HHS identified four plans that a state could choose: (1) one of the three largest plans in the state's small group market health insurance plans; (2) one of the three largest state employee health benefit plans; (3) one of the three largest national plans offered through the Federal Employees Health Benefits Program; or (4) the largest commercial non-Medicaid health maintenance organization operating in the state. If the state does not select a benchmark plan, the state will default to the largest plan by enrollment in the largest product by enrollment in the state's small group market.[26]

States also have the option of requiring QHPs to offer benefits in addition to EHB. If they choose to do so, states must identify which specific state-required benefits are in excess of the EHB. Under HHS regulations, if a state required QHPs to cover benefits beyond EHB on or after January 1, 2012, the state would be responsible for defraying the cost of these services.

States Must Streamline Eligibility and Enrollment Systems

States operating their own exchanges generally must ensure that the exchanges will be able to determine an applicant's eligibility for QHPs, as well as for Medicaid and CHIP.[27] Specifically, under PPACA and implementing regulations, states must establish an electronic, streamlined, and coordinated system through which an individual may apply for and receive a determination of eligibility for enrollment in a QHP,[28] Medicaid, CHIP, or Basic Health Program, if applicable. Exchanges must be able to use a single application that can be completed online, by mail, over the telephone, or in person. This means that no matter how an individual submits an application or which program receives the application, an individual will use the same application and receive an eligibility determination, without the need to submit information to multiple programs. Thus, state IT systems must be interoperable and integrated with an exchange, Medicaid, and CHIP to allow consumers to easily switch from private insurance to Medicaid and CHIP as their circumstances change. Exchanges must also be able to transmit certain data to HHS to be verified before determining applicants' eligibility. HHS, through a "federal data services hub," will coordinate with the Department of Homeland Security, the Internal Revenue Service, and other federal agencies to verify applicant information, such as citizenship and household income. With the amount of data that states must share with HHS in order to verify eligibility, developing streamlined eligibility and enrollment systems is a vast undertaking requiring states to develop sophisticated IT systems.

As part of the enrollment and eligibility process, HHS directs exchanges to rely on existing electronic sources of data to the maximum extent possible to verify relevant information, with high levels of privacy and security protection for consumers. For the majority of applicants, an automated electronic data matching process should eliminate the need for paper documentation.

States Must Conduct Consumer Assistance and Outreach

States that operate their own exchange are required to conduct consumer assistance and outreach through a number of activities. States that partner with HHS may assume some aspects of this function. Specifically, exchanges must have consumer assistance functions that are available to consumers to provide help in using the exchange. Such functions are required to be accessible to individuals with disabilities and individuals with limited English proficiency. Exchanges are also required to operate a toll-free call center and maintain a website that, among other things, allows consumers to compare qualified health plan benefits, costs, and quality ratings, and select and enroll in a plan. Further, exchanges must assist consumers with accessing and obtaining coverage, including providing tools to help consumers access the exchange, determine which plan or program to enroll in, and determine their eligibility for premium tax credits and cost sharing reductions.

As part of states' consumer outreach and assistance activities, each exchange is also required to operate a navigator program, which will provide eligible organizations with grants so they can raise awareness of QHPs' availability and facilitate consumers' selection of QHPs. Navigators may include organizations such as trade associations, community and consumer-focused non-profit groups and chambers of commerce. Navigators must maintain expertise in eligibility, enrollment, and program specifications. The entity serving as a navigator must deliver information to the public in a fair, accurate, and impartial manner that is culturally and linguistically appropriate to the needs of the population they serve.[29] HHS afforded state-based exchanges the opportunity to use in-person assisters in certain circumstances to ensure that the full range of services that the navigator program will provide in subsequent years are provided during the exchanges' initial year of operation. State partnership exchanges in which states will assist with consumer assistance functions will be required to establish and operate an in-person assistance program. While in-person assisters may receive the same training as navigators, they are part of a separate and distinct program and can use establishment grants to fund their operation.

PPACA requires that exchanges regularly consult with certain groups of stakeholders for all activities, including establishing and operating consumer assistance programs. These stakeholders include educated health care consumers enrolled in QHPs, representatives of small businesses and self-employed individuals, advocates for enrolling hardto-reach populations, and individuals and entities with experience in facilitating enrollment in health insurance coverage. Further, HHS provided supplementing guidance on activities states may want to consider as part of their outreach and education, including:[30]

- performing market analysis or an environmental scan to assess outreach and education needs to determine geographic and demographic-based target areas and vulnerable populations for outreach efforts;
- developing a "toolkit" for outreach to include educational materials and information;
- designing a media strategy and other information dissemination tools; and
- submitting a final outreach and education plan to HHS.

States Must Ensure Financial Sustainability of the Exchange

States operating their own exchanges are required to ensure their exchanges will be self-sustaining by 2015—meaning that states must ensure their exchanges have sufficient funding to support ongoing operations.[31] PPACA allows these exchanges to generate funding for exchange operations in certain ways, such as charging user fees or other assessment fees to exchange-participating health insurance issuers. Under HHS guidance, states are to submit a plan to HHS to demonstrate how their exchanges will be financially sustainable by January 1, 2015.

Despite Some Challenges, Selected States Have Taken Action to Establish Exchanges and Report They Will Be Ready for Enrollment by October 2013

Nearly All Selected States Have Created an Operating and Governance Structure

Six of the seven states in our study were conditionally approved by HHS to create a state-based exchange. State exchange officials we interviewed said that, among the reasons that states chose to establish this type of exchange are that it allows the state to (1) maintain consistency between the insurance market inside and outside the exchange, (2) better control its insurance market, and (3) have opportunities to better meet the unique needs of the state's population. In contrast, Iowa officials said the state opted to partner with HHS due to the high cost of building and maintaining a state-based exchange—which the state estimated to be $15.9 million annually. Iowa officials also reported that, by assuming responsibility over certain exchange activities, such as overseeing and certifying qualified health plans, partnering with HHS allows the state to maintain regulatory control over its insurance market. Iowa officials told us that the state plans to transition to a state-based exchange sometime in the future.

To begin building an exchange, six of the seven states have established an operating structure through state legislation or by executive order. As a partnership state, Iowa is not establishing an operating structure at this time because HHS will initially establish and operate the exchange. As Iowa switches to a state-based exchange, it will need to establish an operating structure.

As shown in table 1, states varied in how they established their exchange operating structures. For example, three states—New York, Nevada, and Rhode Island—plan to run their exchange as entities within an existing state agency. Exchange officials in New York told us that basing the exchange within an existing state agency—New York's Department of Health—allows the state to leverage established administrative systems and procedures, thereby relieving the exchange from some of the administrative burdens common to start-up organizations. Table 1 also shows that five out of the six states that have established an exchange have also created a governance board that ranges in member composition and expertise. Consistent with HHS regulation, all five governance boards include members that represent consumer interests.

Table 1. Summary of Exchange Operating and Governance Structures in Selected States

State	Type of exchange	Operating structure	Governance structure
District of Columbia	State-based	Independent authority established by state legislation	11 Board members: 4 non-voting ex officio members (or their designees) and 7 voting members appointed by the mayor with the consent of the council with demonstrated expertise in at least 2 of 12 designated areas, such as health care financing and public health programs; at least 1 member must possess knowledge of health care consumer interest advocacy. An executive director, hired by the board, will direct, administer, and manage the operations of the authority.
Iowa	Partnership	Will defer to HHS	Will defer to HHS
Minnesota	State-based	Board established by state legislationa	7 Board members: the commissioner of Human Services (or a designee) and 6 members appointed by the governor with the consentof both the state Senate and the House of Representatives—1 member representing interests of individual consumers eligible for individual market coverage, 1 member representing individual consumers eligible for public health care program coverage, 1 member representing small employers, 1 member with expertise in health administration and health care finance,

State	Type of exchange	Operating structure	Governance structure
			1 member with expertise in public health and the uninsured, and 1 member representing health policy issues related to small group and individual markets.
Nevada	State-based	Independent public agency established by state legislation	10 Board members: 3 ex officio non-voting members (or their designees) and 7 voting members—5 appointed by the governor, 1 member appointed by the Senate majority leader and 1 member appointed by the speaker of Assembly. The Board has 5 advisory committees: (1) Finance and Sustainability; (2) Plan Certification and Management; (3) Small Business Health Options Program Exchange; (4) Reinsurance and Risk Adjustment; and (5) Consumer Assistance.
New York	State-based	Division within the New York State Department of Health established by executive order	No board created. The New York Health Benefit Exchange established five regional advisory committees to advise and make recommendations on the exchange establishment and operations. Committee members include consumer advocates, small business representatives, health care providers, health plans, agents, brokers, insurers, labor organizations, and policy experts.
Oregon	State-based	Public corporation established by legislationb	9 Board members: 2 ex officio voting members (or their designees) and 7 voting members appointed by the governor with Senate confirmation.cAt least 2 voting members must be: (1) an individual consumer purchasing health care through the exchange; and (2) a small business employer purchasing health care through the exchange.
Rhode Island	State-based	Department within executive department established by executive order	13 Board members, including the director of the Department of Administration; the Health Insurance Commissioner; the Secretary of the executive office of Health and Human Services; the director of the Department of Health; and 9 members appointed by the governor: 2 represent consumer organizations, 2 represent small businesses.dA director of the Division of the Rhode Island Health Benefits Exchange—appointed by the governor—will organize, administer, and manage the operations of the division. No member of the Board is affiliated with a group or organization that has a conflict of interest withthe exchange.

Source: GAO analysis of state legislation and executive orders.

[a]Under Minnesota law, an agency in the executive branch who is authorized to (1) perform administrative acts, (2) issue or revoke licenses or certifications, (3) make rules, or (4) adjudicate contested cases or appeals must be designated as a "board." The Minnesota Insurance Marketplace was established with such authorities.

[b]The Oregon Health Insurance Exchange Corporation is a public corporation performing governmental functions and exercising governmental powers. O.R.S. § 741.001 (2011).

[c]The voting members must collectively offer expertise, knowledge, and experience in individual insurance purchasing, business, finance, sales, health benefits administration, individual and small group health insurance and use of the health insurance exchange.

[d]The board must include a balance of members with expertise in a diverse range of health care areas including, but not limited to, health benefits plan administration, health care finance and accounting, administering a public or private health care delivery system, state employee health purchasing, electronic commerce, and promoting health and wellness.

States Have Taken Steps toward Certifying Qualified Health Plans

All seven states in our review reported taking steps toward certifying QHPs. Two states have decided whether their exchanges will have the authority to actively select which QHPs may participate in the exchange. As active purchasers, exchanges can select QHPs by applying additional criteria and negotiating with health insurance issuers, or by a combination of these actions. As table 2 shows, two states decided to organize their exchanges as active purchasers, while the remaining five states will organize their exchanges as passive purchasers, allowing all plans that meet the minimum requirements for QHPs to participate in the exchange.

To identify benchmark plans, all selected states analyzed the plans and considered various factors, including whether the plans offered by the state required benefits in addition to the EHB required under PPACA. In choosing their benchmark plans, all seven states identified plans that included state-mandated benefits that did not exceed PPACA's EHB requirements. Table 2 shows that five of the seven states recommended benchmark plans to HHS, while two states chose not to identify a benchmark plan and will default to the largest small group plan in their state.

Table 2. Selected States' Insurance Market Organization and Essential Health Benefits (EHB)

State	Market organization	Essential health benefits benchmark plan	Plan type
District of Columbia	passive purchaser	recommended	small group
Iowa	passive purchaser	defaulted	small group
Minnesota	passive purchaser[a]	defaulted	small group
Nevada	passive purchaser	recommended	small group
New York	passive purchaser	recommended	small group
Oregon	active purchaser	recommended	small group
Rhode Island	active purchaser	recommended	small group

Source: GAO analysis of HHS documents and the Henry Kaiser Family Foundation as of January 3, 2013 and March 13, 2013.

[a]According to Minnesota officials, the state expects to organize its market as an active purchaser in 2015.

Definitions: "Recommended" means that a state has recommended an EHB benchmark plan to HHS or developed a preliminary EHB recommendation. "Defaulted" means that a state has not recommended an EHB benchmark plan and will default to the largest small group plan.

All seven states included in our review have taken steps to invite health insurers to participate in their exchanges. For example, in January 2013, New York released an invitation to participate and began accepting applications for licensed insurers in the state (and those expected to be licensed by October 2013) to apply for certain QHPs to be offered through the New York exchange. The exchange governing board will review the applications of individual health plans to make sure they meet all federal minimum participation standards and other requirements to be certified as QHPs. Officials reported that the exchange anticipates certifying plans by mid-July 2013, and will be ready for enrollment on October 1, 2013.

Minnesota and Oregon requested applications in October 2012 from insurers who wanted to offer QHPs in the state's exchange, while the District began accepting applications in April 2013. Insurers certified through the exchange must demonstrate the ability to meet minimum certification requirements including providing adequate networks, care coordination, and quality measures, among other things. Oregon officials told us the state plans to certify QHPs by the summer of 2013 and begin enrolling consumers in October 2013.

States Encountered Time Constraints and Other Challenges, but Are Moving Forward in Simplifying and Streamlining Eligibility and Enrollment Systems

All seven states in our review are in various stages of developing an IT infrastructure that can support a streamlined and integrated eligibility and enrollment system. A major focus of the states' integration activities is redesigning their current Medicaid and CHIP eligibility and enrollment systems. State officials described this as the most significant and onerous aspect of developing an IT infrastructure to support the exchange, given the age and limited functionality of current state systems. All seven states in our review use outdated systems, which lack the capacity to support web-based streamlined processes.

Further, the majority of states operate multiple eligibility and enrollment systems that serve individuals enrolled not only in Medicaid and CHIP but in other public assistance programs, such as Temporary Assistance to Needy Families (TANF) and the Supplemental Nutrition Assistance Program (SNAP). These separate systems, which may be managed by multiple entities across the state, have limited interface capabilities. For example, similar to other states in our review, Oregon operates multiple enrollment and eligibility systems, whereby only a limited amount of enrollee information is accessible and reusable across multiple programs. In addition, Oregon has multiple interfaces between these programs to support integrated business processes, making systems complex, inflexible, and expensive to maintain. To address these kinds of issues, states are using enhanced federal funding, referred to as the 90 percent match, to either upgrade or rebuild their outdated Medicaid and CHIP eligibility and enrollment systems to meet the requirements under PPACA.[32] As states upgrade their Medicaid and CHIP systems, many are also taking the opportunity to integrate enrollment and eligibility processes for other public assistance programs, such as TANF and SNAP, in order to provide shared services across programs.

In addition to upgrading eligibility and enrollment systems, six of the seven states are in various stages of building the exchange IT infrastructure needed to integrate these systems and allow consumers to navigate among health programs and purchase QHPs through a variety of access points, using a single streamlined application.[33] The integrated systems will enable states to collect information needed for eligibility determination and verification, not only from their own state systems, but from federal systems as well. These systems are to utilize a federal data services hub provided by CMS, which will serve as a single source of the federal data that are needed to determine eligibility. To use this system, state systems are to transmit requests for data through the federal data services hub to multiple federal agencies, such as the Department of Homeland Security and the Internal Revenue Service.[34] The federal data services hub is to return the data in near real-time back to the state systems where it can be used to verify the information the states collected for determining applicants' eligibility.

Two states—New York and Oregon—are further along in this work than the other states in our review, as they were awarded early innovator grants to develop an IT infrastructure that will integrate Medicaid, CHIP, and other programs. To develop its state integrated systems, Oregon will use a commercial framework that can be easily adopted and used by other states. As part of its approach and consistent with the intent of the early innovator grant, Oregon has begun working with multiple states to share this framework, including their analyses, design, and other components.

CCIIO officials indicated that readiness testing of states' eligibility and enrollment systems for the exchange will begin in March 2013 and continue through August 2013. To date, three of the states in our review—Nevada, New York and Oregon—have begun testing various aspects of their eligibility, enrollment, and federal data services hub functionality with CCIIO. According to CCIIO officials, the remaining states in our review are expected to begin testing over the next few months. Most state officials told us that because of the complexities of developing an integrated and streamlined eligibility and enrollment system, they plan to use a phased approach to implementation to ensure that key system changes are in place before 2014. Specifically, they will focus first on ensuring that new systems are capable of determining eligibility for enrollment in QHPs, Medicaid, CHIP, and the exchange, and will integrate other assistance programs—such as SNAP and TANF— during later stages.

While state officials reported they expect to be ready to enroll individuals by October 1, 2013 and are moving forward with IT-related efforts, officials in six states identified challenges they faced with developing aspects of their systems, given compressed timeframes and a lack of clear federal requirements related to the federal data services hub. For example, exchange officials expressed concerns about the timeframes for implementation, because of the complexities and large undertaking of integrating and modernizing these systems. Further, most officials reported that transitioning multiple programs into a streamlined and coordinated eligibility and enrollment system could take years to fully implement. Officials in six states told us that developing business rules for the eligibility and enrollment system was challenging because they did not have complete information on the requirements of the federal data services hub. Because of implementation timelines, however, these officials said they needed to begin IT-related activities before receiving complete federal guidance. Most officials reported they were concerned that this could lead to changes late in the development process. To address this uncertainty, a few states built in flexibility in their requests for proposals when making procurement decisions. Officials in one state also reported that, in order to meet timeframes, modifications to the IT systems will be completed in 2014 (after enrollment begins), based on guidance issued late in the development process. CMS has indicated that while the federal data services hub is still under development, CMS has released guidance to the states on how to access or verify data through the federal data services hub through such sources as webinars, conferences, and other forums. Despite the challenges associated with developing the IT systems, officials in six states reported their systems will be ready for enrollment by October 1, 2013.

States Are Developing Outreach and Assistance Programs to Help Consumers Enroll in the Exchange

Six of the seven states included in our review are in various stages of developing a consumer outreach and assistance program to reach out to potential consumers and help them enroll. As a partnership state, Iowa has not yet decided whether and to what extent it will assist HHS with aspects of this function. Most states have contracted with or plan to contract with vendors to design a program. The vendors will assist with the exchanges' branding, which will be able to translate materials into multiple languages and take into account the needs of individuals with disabilities. The vendors will also design and implement communications and marketing plans (for example, radio and television ads) with the goal of enrolling the maximum number of eligible individuals into the exchange.

As part of the consumer outreach and assistance programs, states will use a range of tools to provide potential consumers with information and assist them in enrolling in an exchange. These include:

Navigators and in-person assistors. Six of the seven states in our review plan to use navigators and assistors to provide in-person enrollment assistance to individuals applying for health insurance, such as assisting individuals with selecting QHPs or providing information to individuals in a way that is culturally and linguistically appropriate. HHS plans to assume responsibility for operating the navigator program in Iowa, since it is a partnership state. Nearly all states told us that assistance will need to be tailored to the unique needs of their populations. For example, Nevada officials told us that their program must be able to accommodate individuals who live in Nevada's remote frontier region, where population density can be as low as two people per square mile and which may lack infrastructure such as Internet access. New York officials told us they will address linguistic and cultural challenges reaching individuals in some of New York City's more diverse communities.

Four states—the District, New York, Oregon, and Rhode Island—plan to leverage state resources within existing health and human services programs to support navigators and assistors. For example, Oregon plans to model its navigator program after a state Medicaid program that provides uninsured individuals with premium assistance and access to health care information and resources. Similarly, New York, which issued a request for application in February 2013 for in-person assistors and navigators, will model its approach after its community assistance programs and will provide assistance through a variety of access points in other local areas across the state. New York officials told us that the state plans to sign contracts with navigators and in-person assistors in the summer of 2013 and begin training them in August or September 2013.

Web portals and call centers. Six of the seven states in our review are designing web portals and contact centers as part of their consumer assistance and outreach initiatives. The seventh state, Iowa, is a partnership state and is deferring this responsibility to HHS. State planning documents in the remaining six states indicated that the web portals and the contact centers will be central to assisting residents. State officials told us that web portals, in particular, will ease comparisons among health plans by providing standardized information about each health plan's premium, benefit structure, and cost-sharing provisions. For example, District officials told us that a web portal, which is being developed in conjunction with the IT infrastructure, will be the key access point for consumers to interface with the exchange. Similarly, Minnesota is designing a contact center that will offer multiple modes of assistance through such means as Internet access, telephone, mail, and in-person assistance. State officials told us they expect the customer service functions will be ready to operate on October 1, 2013.

States Are Planning for Long-Term Sustainability with Multiple Revenue Options, but Faced Uncertainties Estimating Costs

Officials in six states in our review reported they are considering a number of revenue options for financially sustaining their exchange.[35] For example, as part of the planning efforts to develop these options, three states—Nevada, Minnesota, and the District—created work groups to recommend options for achieving long-term sustainability. In particular, both Minnesota and Nevada created working groups intended to review and propose financing options to enable the exchange to be self-sustaining by January 1, 2015.

While states reported they are considering options to fund ongoing exchange costs, such as salaries and benefits, consulting services, outreach and marketing, and information technology, three states will charge fees to insurance carriers participating in the exchange. Specifically:

- Oregon will charge an administrative fee to insurance carriers participating in the exchange. In particular, carriers will be required to pay a percentage of the premiums (up to 5 percent) based on the number of enrollees in the exchange. The fee is designed to decrease as enrollment in the exchange increases. For example, if more than 300,000 individuals enroll in the exchange, the state exchange will charge carriers up to a 3 percent fee. If enrollment is at or below 175,000, the state exchange will charge carriers up to a 5 percent fee. Between 100,000 and 120,000 enrollees would be required for the exchange to be self-sustaining using the maximum administrative fee of 5 percent. Further, any excess revenues generated above the cost of operating the exchange may be placed in a reserve fund of up to 6 months of operating expenses or returned to insurance carriers.
- Nevada plans to charge insurance carriers a per member per month fee based on enrollment. In its financial sustainability plan, the state estimated the fee will amount to between $7.13 and $7.78 per member per month, which the state anticipates insurance carriers will build into their QHP premiums. In addition, based on the state's estimates, the state expects the fee will be paid by the advance premium tax credit. Nevada is also considering other potential sources of supplementary revenue, such as fees charged for standalone vision and dental plans.
- Minnesota plans to charge an administrative fee to insurance carriers participating in the exchange. Specifically, insurers will be required to

pay a percentage of the premiums (about 3.5 percent) sold through the exchange. The fee will be based on the volume of insurance premiums for plans sold through the exchange.

While the states in our review have developed financing options, some state officials identified challenges with developing these options, given uncertainties related to exchange enrollment. Specifically, financial sustainability will be highly dependent on the size of enrollment and the take up rate, which is the percent of individuals that are estimated to enroll in coverage out of the entire eligible population. Some state officials reported that, estimating enrollment patterns without the benefit of historical data from the exchange, could impact revenue projections. Further, according to one state, uptake estimates among various groups are “drastically different,” so that estimating enrollment could result in significantly different per member per month carrier fees required to fund the exchange. Officials from two states reported that given these uncertainties, they expect to make adjustments to these estimates over time.

AGENCY COMMENTS

We provided a draft of this report to the Secretary of HHS for review and comment. In response, HHS provided technical comments, which we incorporated as appropriate. Additionally, we provided excerpts of the draft report to exchange officials, such as the executive director and chief policy research and evaluation officer, in the seven states we interviewed for this study. We incorporated their technical comments as appropriate.

Sincerely yours,
Stanley J. Czerwinski
Director, Strategic Issues

APPENDIX I: OBJECTIVES, SCOPE AND METHODOLOGY

This report addresses the following objectives: (1) identify states' responsibilities for establishing health benefit exchanges; and (2) describe the actions selected states have taken to establish exchanges and the challenges they have encountered.[1]

To identify states' responsibilities for establishing exchanges and the challenges they encountered, we reviewed selected Patient Protection and Affordable Care Act (PPACA) provisions and Department of Health and Human Services (HHS) implementing regulations and guidance related to the following categories:

- establishing a governance and operating structure;
- ensuring exchanges will be capable of certifying qualified health plans;
- simplifying and streamlining eligibility and enrollment systems;
- conducting consumer assistance and outreach; and
- ensuring the financial sustainability of the exchange.

Our review of HHS's guidance included HHS's blueprint for approval of state-based and partnership exchanges, information bulletins, questions and answers, and webinars. We also reviewed reports that have summarized state responsibilities with regard to the categories we included in our study, including those completed by federal agencies monitoring the implementation process and national associations that play a role in assisting states with implementation. Specifically, we reviewed reports from the Congressional Budget Office, the Congressional Research Service, and relevant state associations, such as the National Association of Insurance Commissioners, the National Conference of State Legislatures, the National Association of State Budget Officers, and the National Academy for State Health Policy.

To identify actions selected states have taken to create exchanges and the challenges they encountered, we conducted semistructured interviews with officials in seven states: the District of Columbia,[2] Iowa, Minnesota, Nevada, New York, Oregon, and Rhode Island. We selected these states on the basis of:

1. The percentage of the uninsured population in states based on a 3-year average (2008 to 2010);
2. The percentage of the uninsured population in states in 2011;
3. The amount of exchange grants awarded to states on a per capita basis;[3]
4. Geographic dispersion; and
5. The type of exchange states intended to establish, based on data publicly available as of September 27, 2012.[4]

Table 3 shows the characteristics of the states selected for our review. We initially selected two states that intended to operate as federally facilitated exchanges—Florida and Maine. However, exchange officials in both states declined to be interviewed. Therefore, this review focused on states' responsibilities to establish state-based and partnership exchanges.

Table 3. Characteristics of States Included in GAO Study

Selected States	Percentage of the uninsured population based on 3-year average	Percentage of the uninsured population in 2011	Exchange grants awarded on a per capita basis as of September 27, 2012	Census region	Status of intended state action, as of September 27, 2012
District of Columbia	11.4%	8.4%	$136.6	South	State-based
Iowa	10.7	10	11.6	Midwest	Studying options
Minnesota	8.7	9.2	13.9	Midwest	Studying options
Nevada	20	22.6	27.7	West	State-based
New York	14.2	12.2	9.5	Northeast	State-based
Oregon	16.5	13.8	16.9	West	State-based
Rhode Island	11.5	12	61.5	Northeast	State-based
Floridaa	20.7	19.8	0	South	Federally facilitated
Maineb	9.9	10	0.8	Northeast	Federally facilitated

Source: GAO analysis of U.S. Census Bureau and HHS data.

[a] Florida was initially selected for inclusion in our review based on our selection criteria noted, but exchange officials declined to be interviewed for our study.

[b] Maine was initially selected for inclusion in our review based on our selection criteria noted, but exchange officials declined to be interviewed for our study.

We conducted initial interviews in person and by telephone between October and November 2012 and follow-up interviews between February and March 2013. The interview questions focused on states' actions regarding establishing an exchange and the challenges they encountered in the following areas: establishing an operating and governance structure, developing information technology systems and infrastructure to support a streamlined eligibility and enrollment system, ensuring exchanges will be capable of certifying qualified health plans, creating consumer outreach and assistance, and ensuring the exchange's financial sustainability. We also met with budget officials in some of the states to discuss the fiscal aspects of establishing exchanges, including how states will ensure exchanges are financially sustainable. The responses to the interviews are not intended to be representative of all state exchange and budget officials.

To supplement our interviews, we reviewed state planning, budget, and implementation documents, such as state blueprint applications, business plans, exchange grant applications, and contracting documents.

In addition, we conducted interviews with officials from the Centers for Medicare & Medicaid Services (CMS) and CMS's Center for Consumer Information and Insurance Oversight and relevant state associations, including the National Association of State Budget Officers, National Conference of State Legislatures and the National Association of Insurance Commissioners.

We conducted our work from September 2011 to April 2013 in accordance with generally accepted government audit standards. Those standards require that we plan and perform the audit to obtain sufficient, appropriate evidence to provide a reasonable basis for our findings and conclusions based on our audit objectives. We believe that the evidence obtained provides a reasonable basis for our findings and conclusions based on our audit objectives.

End Notes

[1] Pub. L. No. 111-148, 124 Stat. 119 (Mar. 23, 2010) (PPACA), as amended by the Health Care and Education Reconciliation Act, (HCERA) Pub. L. No. 111-152,124 Stat.1029 (Mar. 30, 2010). In this report, references to PPACA include any amendments made by HCERA.

[2] Pub. L. No. 111-148, § 1311(b), 124 Stat. at 173.

[3] PPACA requires the establishment of a Small Business Health Options Program, or SHOP—exchanges where small employers can shop for and purchase coverage for their employees. Under PPACA, until 2016, states have the option to define "small employers" either as those with 100 or fewer employees or 50 or fewer employees. Beginning in 2016, small employers will be defined as those with 100 or fewer employees. Beginning in 2017, states may allow large employers to obtain coverage through an exchange (but will not be required to do so). For purposes of our review, we did not include SHOP exchanges in the scope of our work.

[4] Medicaid is a joint federal-state program that finances health care coverage for certain categories of low-income individuals.

[5] CHIP is a federal state program which provides health care coverage to children 18 years of age and younger living in low-income families whose incomes exceed the eligibility requirements for Medicaid.

[6] Pub. L. No. 111-148, § 1413(c), 124 Stat. at 234.

[7] A partnership exchange is a variation of a federally facilitated exchange. HHS will establish and operate this type of exchange with states assisting HHS to carry out certain functions of that exchange.

[8] For purposes of this report, we focused on certain categories of responsibilities. Therefore, this list does not include all states' responsibilities related to creating and operating an exchange.

[9] Specifically, we selected states on the basis of whether they intended to establish a state-based, federally facilitated, or partnership exchange, as of September 27, 2012. At that time, states had not yet formally declared their intention to HHS. We used the most readily available information at that time from HHS and the Kaiser Family Foundation.

[10] Beginning on January 1, 2014, a premium tax credit will be available to help eligible tax filers and their dependents pay for qualified health plans purchased through PPACA exchanges. The premium tax credit is available on an advance basis, referred to as advance payments of the premium tax credit, and any advance payments are reconciled on a tax filer's tax return. Ultimately, tax credits will be calculated using income reported on tax returns. The credits will generally be available to eligible tax filers and their dependents who are (1) enrolled in one or more qualified health plans through an exchange, and (2) not eligible for other health insurance coverage. More specifically, to qualify for the premium tax credit, an individual or family must generally have income between 100 and 400 percent of the federal poverty level and not qualify for other health care coverage, such as Medicare, Medicaid, or employer-sponsored coverage that meets a minimum value standard specified in PPACA.

[11] PPACA provides cost sharing subsidies to certain individuals to help them pay for costs related to the use of health services. Cost sharing generally refers to costs that an individual must pay when using services that are covered under the health plan that the person is enrolled in. Common forms of cost sharing include copayments and deductibles.

[12] The Basic Health Program (BHP) is an alternative to qualified health plans under which states may offer subsidized coverage to non-elderly individuals with incomes between 133 and 200 percent of the federal poverty level who are otherwise not eligible for other types of coverage such as affordable employer-sponsored insurance or traditional Medicaid. For operating this program, states will receive federal funding equivalent to 95 percent of the premium tax credits and cost sharing reductions that would apply to individuals if they were enrolled in exchange plans.

[13] PPACA requires states to establish exchanges by January 1, 2014. Pub. L. No. 111- 148, § 1311(b), 124 Stat. 173. The Secretary of HHS must establish and operate an exchange in states that do not elect to operate an exchange or in states where the Secretary determines, by January 1, 2013, that a state has failed to take actions necessary to establish an exchange. Pub. L. No. 111-148, § 1321(c), 124 Stat. 186. Through subsequent guidance, HHS has identified options for states to partner with HHS when HHS establishes and operates an exchange. Specifically, under this model

[14] These grants were awarded to states in 2010 and 2011, and are no longer being awarded. These grants provided one year of funding and a state could receive only one grant.

[15] There are two types of establishment grants. Level I establishment grants, awarded to states in 2010, were available to all states, whether they were developing a state-based exchange or participating in a partnership exchange or a federally facilitated exchange. These grants

provided for one year of funding, and a state could apply for multiple grants. Level II establishment grants, awarded on a quarterly basis through 2015, are available only to states that create a state-based exchange and are moving ahead at a faster pace.

[16] As noted earlier, for purposes of this report, we refer to the District of Columbia as a state.

[17] One state, Alaska, did not apply for and was not awarded exchange grant funding.

[18] As of March 27, 2013, certain states had returned this funding to HHS for reasons such as the state's decision not to pursue a state-based exchange.

[19] Qualified individuals must reside in the state in which the exchange is offered and include U.S. citizens and legal immigrants who are not incarcerated.

[20] A state exchange may contract with an eligible entity, including a state Medicaid agency or any other state agency, incorporated under and subject to the laws of at least one state, that has demonstrated experience on a state or regional basis in the individual and small group health insurance markets and in benefits coverage, but is not an issuer.

[21] CMS will work with states participating in state partnership exchanges to ensure that such guidance is consistent with federal regulatory standards and operational timelines. CMS anticipates that states will choose to use the National Association of Insurance Commissioners' System for Electronic Rate and Form Filing to collect and review QHP data. The state will review issuer applications for QHP certification for compliance with the standards and will provide a certification recommendation for each QHP to CMS. CMS will review and confirm the state's recommendations, coordinate plan preview, make final certification decisions, and make available certified QHP plans in the exchange for the relevant state partnership exchange. CMS will work closely with states in state partnership exchanges to coordinate this process.

[22] "Good standing" generally means that the insurer has no outstanding sanctions imposed by a state's department of insurance.

[23] Under PPACA, states may require plans to offer benefits in addition to these categories. States are required to either make payments to individual enrollees or to the issuers to defray the costs of these additional benefits.

[24] Pub. L. No. 111-148, §§ 1302 (d), 10104(b)(1), 124 Stat. 167, 896. Accordingly, the actuarial value of a plan represents the expected percentage of costs the plan will incur for the EHB services provided to a standard population. For example, a gold plan with an 80 percent actuarial value would be expected to pay, on average, 80 percent of a standard population's expected medical expenses for the EHB. The individuals covered by the plan would be expected to pay, on average, the remaining 20 percent of the expected cost-sharing expenses in the form of deductibles, copayments, and coinsurance.

[25] Each state's benchmark plan will apply to their respective exchanges for plan years 2014 and 2015, while HHS will revisit this issue for the 2016 plan year.

[26] The term "small group market health plan" is defined as the health insurance market in which employers with 100 or fewer employees offer group health plans.

[27] States with either state-based exchanges or partnership exchanges have the option of (1) allowing exchanges to make eligibility determinations for Medicaid and CHIP or (2) having exchanges make an assessment, with the state Medicaid agency or other relevant state agency making the actual determinations of eligibility. In addition, PPACA and implementing regulations provide for states, regardless of whether they are establishing an exchange, to create a transitional reinsurance program for 2014 through 2016 to help stabilize premiums for coverage in the individual market. HHS will establish a reinsurance program for any state that fails to establish this program. Further, beginning with the 2014 benefit year, each state electing to operate an exchange may establish a permanent risk

adjustment program for all non-grandfathered plans in the individual and small group market both inside and outside of the exchanges. HHS will establish this risk adjustment program for any state that will not operate an exchange or for states operating an exchange but which do not elect to administer the risk adjustment program. These risk-spreading mechanisms are designed to mitigate the potential impact of adverse selection and provide stability for health insurance issuers in the individual and small group markets. We did not include states' reinsurance and risk adjustment activities in the scope of our work.

[28] In determining eligibility for a QHP, exchanges must also determine whether applicants qualify for premium tax credits or cost sharing reductions for these plans. States electing to establish and operate state-based exchanges, however, may choose to rely on HHS to make these determinations.

[29] Unlike insurance agents and brokers, navigators are not authorized to receive compensation or other forms of payment—either directly or indirectly—from any health insurance issuer in connection with the enrollment of any qualified individuals, or employees of a qualified employer, in a QHP.

[30] HHS, *Cooperative Agreement to Support Establishment of State-Operated Health Insurance Exchanges*, January 20, 2011.

[31] PPACA prohibits the awarding of establishment grants for exchanges after January 1, 2015. HHS has clarified, however, that states seeking federal funding to establish exchanges may be awarded such funds until December 31, 2014.

[32] States may receive an enhanced administrative federal match—90 percent—for the design, development, and installation or enhancement of eligibility determination systems until December 31, 2015. In order to qualify for the 90 percent match, states must submit an advanced planning document to CMS for review and approval. As part of its review, CMS must determine that the design, development, installation, or enhancement of a state's eligibility system meets a number of standards and conditions, including seamless coordination with the health insurance exchanges. The 90 percent match is available only for costs incurred after April 19, 2011, and before December 31, 2015. Beginning April 19, 2011, states may also qualify for a 75 percent match for the operation of eligibility systems that continue to meet applicable standards and conditions. This enhanced match is not available for systems that do not meet these requirements by December 31, 2015.

[33] As a partnership state, Iowa is not required to establish an exchange infrastructure.

[34] Other federal agencies include the Social Security Administration, the Veteran's Heath Administration, Tricare, the Peace Corps, the Office of Personnel Management, and CMS.

[35] As a partnership exchange, Iowa is not responsible for carrying out this key function.

End Notes for Appendix I

[1] For purposes of this report, we focus on certain categories of responsibilities. Therefore, this list does not include all states' responsibilities related to establishing an exchange.

[2] For ease of reporting and for purposes of this review, we refer to the District of Columbia as a state.

[3] We calculated the amount of total planning, establishment, and early innovator grants awarded on a per capita basis in each state as of September 27, 2012. We divided the total amount of grants awarded to states by the total state population.

[4] Specifically, we selected states on the basis of whether they intended to opt for a state-based, federally facilitated, or partnership exchange as of September 27, 2012. At that time, states had not yet formally declared their intention to HHS through the blueprint application. However, we used the most readily available information at that time from HHS and the Henry Kaiser Family Foundation.

In: States' Establishment of Health Insurance … ISBN: 978-1-62808-575-4
Editors: F. C. Lewis and E. O. Walker

Chapter 2

STATUS OF FEDERAL FUNDING FOR STATE IMPLEMENTATION OF HEALTH INSURANCE EXCHANGES*

Annie L. Mach, Alex C. Engler and C. Stephen Redhead

SUMMARY

The Patient Protection and Affordable Care Act (ACA, P.L. 111-148, as amended) requires health insurance exchanges to be established in every state by January 1, 2014. ACA intends exchanges to be marketplaces where individuals and small businesses can "shop" for health insurance coverage. An exchange may be established by the state itself as a state-based exchange;

otherwise, an exchange will be established by the Secretary of Health and Human Services (HHS) as either a partnership exchange, whereby a state partners with HHS to establish and administer an exchange, or as a federally facilitated exchange wholly operated and administered by HHS.

ACA provided an indefinite appropriation for HHS grants to states to support the planning and establishment of exchanges. For each fiscal year, the HHS Secretary is to determine the total amount that will be made available to each state for exchange grants. No grant may be awarded after January 1, 2015.

---

* This is an edited, reformatted and augmented version of a Congressional Research Service publication, CRS Report for Congress R43066, prepared for Members and Committees of Congress, from www.crs.gov, dated May 8, 2013.

There are three different types of exchanges grants. First, planning grants were awarded to 49 states, the District of Columbia, and four territories. These grants of about $1 million each were intended to provide resources to states to help them plan their health insurance exchanges. Three states returned all or a portion of those funds. Second, there have been multiple rounds of exchange establishment grants. There are two levels of exchange establishment grants: level one establishment grants are awarded to states that have made some progress using their planning funds, and level two establishment grants are designed to provide funding to states that are farther along in the establishment of an exchange. Finally, HHS awarded seven early innovator grants to states (including one award to a consortium of New England states) to support the design and implementation of the information technology systems needed to operate the exchanges. Three states returned their early innovator grant funds.

To date, HHS has awarded a total of $3.8 billion to states and the District of Columbia (DC) in planning, establishment, and early innovator grants.

INTRODUCTION

This report summarizes key federal activities related to the establishment of health insurance exchanges, as required by the Patient Protection and Affordable Care Act (ACA).[1] This report begins with a brief discussion of exchanges, and then *Table 1* summarizes regulatory activity related to exchanges, and *Table 2* shows key implementation dates as established in ACA and in regulations and other guidance documents. *Figure 1* and *Table 3* provide information about the federal grant funds that have been awarded to states for exchange planning and establishment.

HEALTH INSURANCE EXCHANGES

ACA requires health insurance exchanges to be established in every state by January 1, 2014. ACA exchanges are marketplaces where individuals and small employers can shop for and enroll in health insurance coverage. Exchanges are intended to simplify the experience of providing and obtaining coverage in the nongroup and small group markets. They are not intended to supplant the private market outside of exchanges, and individuals and small businesses cannot be compelled to obtain coverage through an exchange. Plans offered in exchanges are generally subject to certain ACA requirements.[2]

An exchange may be established by the state itself as a state-based exchange; otherwise, an exchange will be established by the Secretary of Health and Human Services (HHS) as either a partnership exchange, whereby a state partners with HHS to establish and administer an exchange, or as a federally facilitated exchange wholly operated and administered by HHS.[3] ACA provides general direction regarding the establishment and administration of health insurance exchanges and directs federal agencies, particularly HHS, to promulgate regulations that provide further guidance. For example, § 1321 requires the HHS Secretary to promulgate regulations relating to the establishment and operation of exchanges, the offering of health insurance plans through an exchange, the establishment of programs created by the ACA to mitigate risk in the exchanges, and any other requirements the HHS Secretary deems appropriate. Federal agencies have promulgated a number of final (or interim final) and proposed regulations related to exchange establishment (*Table 1*).

Provisions in ACA, its implementing regulations, and other guidance produced by HHS identify dates by which certain requirements must be met in order for exchanges to be in operation in every state on January 1, 2014, as the law requires. *Table 2* summarizes these key dates.

Health Insurance Exchange Grants

Section 1311 of ACA appropriated indefinite (i.e., unspecified) amounts for planning and establishment grants for health insurance exchanges, which must be operational by the beginning of 2014. For each fiscal year, the HHS Secretary is to determine the total amount that will be made available to each state for exchange grants. However, no grant may be awarded after January 1, 2015.

The subsequent sections discuss the three different types of exchange grants HHS has awarded. *Figure 1* shows the total amount of funding each state has received from exchange planning and establishment grants as well as the type of exchange (state-based, partnership, or federally facilitated) each state intends to have in 2014. *Table 3* shows the amount each state has received from the various types of grants.

Table 1. Recent Regulatory Action Related to Health Insurance Exchanges

Regulation	Federal Agency	Date Published in Federal Register
Final rule on standards related to reinsurance, risk corridors, and risk adjustment, effective May 22, 2012.	HHS	March 23, 2012 (77 Fed. Reg. 17220)
Final rule on Medicaid eligibility changes under ACA, effective January 1, 2014. [Certain provisions of the rule were issued as interim final; comments were due May 7, 2012.]	Centers for Medicare & Medicaid Services, HHS	March 23, 2012 (77 Fed. Reg. 17144)
Final rule on health insurance premium tax credit, effective May 23, 2012.	Internal Revenue Service, Department of the Treasury	May 23, 2012 (77 Fed. Reg. 30377)
Final rule on establishment of exchanges and qualified health plans, and exchange standards for employers, effective May 29, 2012. [Certain provisions of the rule were issued as interim final; comments were due by May 11, 2012.]	HHS	March 27, 2012 (77 Fed. Reg. 18310)
Final rule on standards related to essential health benefits, actuarial value, and accreditation, effective April 26, 2013.	HHS	February 25, 2013 (78 Fed. Reg. 12834)
Final rule on parameters related to: reinsurance, risk corridors, and risk adjustment; cost-sharing reductions; user fees for a federally facilitated exchange; advance payments of the premium tax credits; a federally facilitated Small Business Health Option Program (SHOP); and the medical loss ratio (MLR) program, effective April 30, 2013.	Centers for Medicare & Medicaid Services, HHS	March 11, 2013 (78 Fed. Reg. 15410)
Proposed rule on essential health benefits in alternative benefit plans, eligibility notices, and fair hearing and appeal processes for Medicaid and exchange eligibility appeals. Comments were accepted until February 13, 2013.	Centers for Medicare & Medicaid Services, HHS	January 22, 2013 (78 Fed. Reg. 4594)
Proposed rule on the SHOP exchange under ACA. Comments were accepted until April 1, 2013.	Centers for Medicare & Medicaid Services, HHS	March 11, 2013 (78 Fed. Reg. 15553)

Source: Table prepared by Congressional Research Service based on information collected from the Federal Register.

Table 2. Key Exchange Implementation Dates

Date	Requirement
December 14, 2012	States seeking to establish a state exchange must submit a declaration letter and an exchange blueprint application no later than this date to be considered for exchange approval by January 1, 2013.
January 1, 2013	Each state exchange must be approved to operate by HHS no later than this date in order to be operational on January 1, 2014.[a]
February 15, 2013	States seeking to establish a partnership exchange effective in 2014 must submit a declaration letter and an exchange blueprint application no later than this date.
October 1, 2013	Open enrollment must begin for coverage offered through an exchange for the 2014 coverage year.
January 1, 2014	Exchanges must be established and offer coverage in every state.

Source: Table prepared by Congressional Research Service based on information collected from (1) ACA (P.L. 111-148, as amended); (2) 77 Federal Register 18310; and (3) Letter from Kathleen Sebelius, Secretary of Health and Human Services, to State Governors, November 9, 2012, http://cciio.cms.gov/Archive/TechnicalImplementation-Letters/exchange-blueprint

[a] As of April 8, 2013, HHS has conditionally approved 17 states and the District of Columbia (DC) to operate state exchanges, and seven states have been conditionally approved to operate partnership exchanges. For more information, see http://cciio.cms.gov/resources

Health Insurance Exchange Grants

Section 1311 of ACA appropriated indefinite (i.e., unspecified) amounts for planning and establishment grants for health insurance exchanges, which must be operational by the beginning of 2014. For each fiscal year, the HHS Secretary is to determine the total amount that will be made available to each state for exchange grants. However, no grant may be awarded after January 1, 2015.

The subsequent sections discuss the three different types of exchange grants HHS has awarded. *Figure 1* shows the total amount of funding each state has received from exchange planning and establishment grants as well as the type of exchange (state-based, partnership, or federally facilitated) each state intends to have in 2014. *Table 3* shows the amount each state has received from the various types of grants.

Exchange Planning Grants

Exchange planning grants were given to 49 states, the District of Columbia (DC), and four territories.[4] These grants of about $1 million each were intended to provide resources to states to help them conduct the research and planning needed to determine how their exchanges would be administered and operated. Three states have returned all (Florida and Louisiana) or a portion (New Hampshire) of their exchange planning grants.

Exchange Establishment Grants

There are two levels of exchange establishment grants. Level one establishment grants provide up to one year of funding to states that have made some progress under their exchange planning grants. States may seek an additional year of level one funding in order to meet the criteria necessary to apply for level two funds. Level two establishment grants are designed to provide funding through December 31, 2014, to states that are farther along in the establishment of an exchange. States applying for level two establishment grants must meet specific eligibility criteria regarding the structure and governance of the exchange they are developing. There are a series of deadlines throughout 2013 and 2014 for applying for the level one and level two exchange establishment grants.

HHS has announced seven rounds of exchange establishment grant awards, the most recent of which was on April 8, 2013.[5] To date, 35 states and DC have received a total of approximately $3.6 billion in exchange establishment grant funding.[6] Within that group, 12 states—California, Connecticut, Hawaii, Kentucky, Maryland, Massachusetts, Nevada, New York, Oregon, Rhode Island, Vermont, and Washington—and DC have received both level one and level two funds.

Early Innovator Grants

On February 16, 2011, HHS announced that it was awarding seven grants to help a group of "early innovator" states design and implement the information technology (IT) infrastructure needed to operate health insurance exchanges.[7] The goal is for these states to develop exchange IT models that can be adopted and implemented by other states. Six states and a consortium of New England states received a total of $249 million in early innovator grant funding. Three states—Kansas, Oklahoma, and Wisconsin—have since returned their early innovator grants.

Additional Information

The Center for Consumer Information and Insurance Oversight (CCIIO) at CMS is responsible for implementing ACA's private health insurance reforms and administering the grant programs discussed above. Detailed information on the grants, including funding opportunity announcements, guidance, news releases, and amounts awarded, is available on CCIIO's website.[8]

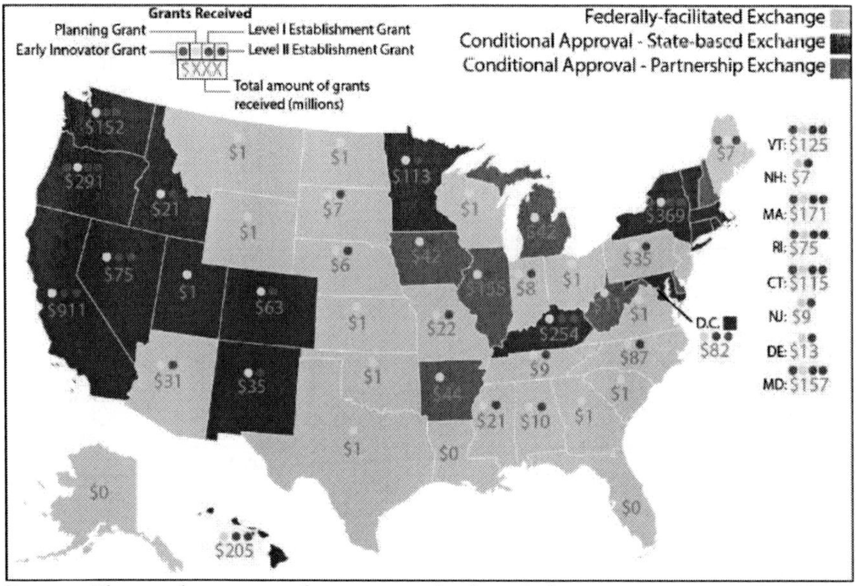

Source: The total amount of grants received and the grant types are based on information from Table 3 of this report. Information about the type of exchange that will be established in each state for 2014 is available from the Center for Consumer Information and Insurance Oversight's (CCIIO) website, at http://cciio.cms.gov/resources/factsheets/state-marketplaces.html.

Notes: The total amount of grants received by each state is rounded to the nearest million. A $0 amount in a state indicates that the state has either not received any grants (Alaska) or has returned all funds received from grants to the federal government (Florida and Louisiana).

The early innovator grant awarded to the University of Massachusetts Medical School is for a multi-state consortium, which includes Connecticut, Maine, Massachusetts, Rhode Island, and Vermont. Each of these states has a green dot in Figure 1 indicating receipt of an early innovator grant; however, the awarded funds are only included in the funding total for Massachusetts.

Figure 1. ACA Exchange Funding to States (As of April 8, 2013).

Table 3. ACA Exchange Funding to States and Territories (As of April 8, 2013) Funding in Dollars

		Health Insurance Exchange Grants			
		Establishment Grants			
State/Territory	Planning	Level I	Level II	Early Innovator	Total
Alabama	1,180,312	8,592,139	NA	NA	9,772,451
Alaska	NA	NA	NA	NA	NA
Arizona	999,670	29,877,427	NA	NA	30,877,097
Arkansas	1,200,928	42,731,407	NA	NA	43,932,335
California	1,000,000	235,901,012	673,705,358	NA	910,606,370
Colorado	1,247,599	61,437,747	NA	NA	62,685,346
Connecticut	996,850	6,687,933	107,358,676	NA[a]	115,043,459
Delaware	1,000,000	11,936,639	NA	NA	12,936,636
DC	1,000,000	8,200,716	72,985,333	NA	82,186,049
Florida	0[b]	NA	NA	NA	0
Georgia	1,000,000	NA	NA	NA	1,000,000
Hawaii	1,000,000	76,255,636	128,086,634	NA	205,342,270
Idaho	1,000,000	20,376,556	NA	NA	21,376,556
Illinois	1,071,784	153,741,352	NA	NA	154,813,136
Indiana	1,000,000	6,895,126	NA	NA	7,895,126
Iowa	1,000,000	41,221,578	NA	NA	42,221,578
Kansas	1,000,000	NA	NA	0[c]	1,000,000
Kentucky	1,000,000	69,990,613	182,707,738	NA	253,698,351
Louisiana	0[d]	NA	NA	NA	0
Maine	1,000,000	5,877,676	NA	NA[a]	6,877,676
Maryland	999,227	27,186,749	123,048,693	6,227,454	157,462,123
Massachusetts	1,000,000	53,324,443	81,256,970	35,591,333[a]	171,172,746
Michigan	999,772	40,517,249	NA	NA	41,517,021
Minnesota	1,000,000	112,169,007	NA	NA	113,169,007
Mississippi	1,000,000	20,143,618	NA	NA	21,143,618
Missouri	1,000,000	20,865,716	NA	NA	21,865,716
Montana	1,000,000	NA	NA	NA	1,000,000
Nebraska	1,000,000	5,481,838	NA	NA	6,481,838
Nevada	1,000,000	23,738,273	50,016,012	NA	74,754,285
New Hampshire	334,000[e]	6,267,088	NA	NA	6,601,088
New Jersey	1,223,186	7,674,130	NA	NA	8,897,316
New Mexico	1,000,000	34,279,483	NA	NA	35,279,483
New York	1,000,000	154,746,207	185,822,357	27,431,432	368,999,996
North Carolina	1,000,000	86,357,315	NA	NA	87,357,315
North Dakota	1,000,000	NA	NA	NA	1,000,000
Ohio	1,000,000	NA	NA	NA	1,000,000
Oklahoma	1,000,000	NA	NA	0[f]	1,000,000
Oregon	1,000,000	15,652,301	226,472,074	48,096,307	291,220,682
Pennsylvania	1,000,000	33,832,212	NA	NA	34,832,212
Rhode Island	1,000,000	15,063,314	58,515,871	NA[a]	74,579,185
South Carolina	1,000,000	NA	NA	NA	1,000,000

		Health Insurance Exchange Grants			
		Establishment Grants			
State/Territory	Planning	Level I	Level II	Early Innovator	Total
South Dakota	1,000,000	5,879,569	NA	NA	6,879,569
Tennessee	1,000,000	8,110,165	NA	NA	9,110,165
Texas	1,000,000	NA	NA	NA	1,000,000
Utah	1,000,000	NA	NA	NA	1,000,000
Vermont	1,000,000	20,258,116	104,178,965	NA[a]	125,437,081
Virginia	1,000,000	NA	NA	NA	1,000,000
Washington	996,285	22,942,671	127,852,056	NA	151,791,012
West Virginia	1,000,000	9,667,694	NA	NA	10,667,694
Wisconsin	999,873	NA	NA	0[g]	999,873
Wyoming	800,000	NA	NA	NA	800,000
Total: 50 States & DC	48,049,486	1,503,880,715	2,122,006,737	117,346,526	3,791,283,464
Puerto Rico	917,205	NA	NA	NA	917,205
Virgin Islands	1,000,000	NA	NA	NA	1,000,000
Guam	1,000,000	NA	NA	NA	1,000,000
American Samoa	1,000,000	NA	NA	NA	1,000,000
Northern Marianas	NA	NA	NA	NA	NA
Total: All	51,966,691	1,503,880,715	2,122,006,737	117,346,526	3,795,200,669

Source: Table prepared by Congressional Research Service based on (1) grant award announcements and other information provided by the Center for Consumer Information and Insurance Oversight (CCIIO) at http://cciio.cms.gov/Archive/Grants/exchanges-map.html; and (2) data compiled in the HHS Tracking Accountability in Government Grants Systems (TAGGS) at http://taggs.hhs.gov.

Notes: NA = not applicable (i.e., state/territory has not applied for or received funding).

[a] The early innovator grant awarded to the University of Massachusetts Medical School is for a multi-state consortium, which includes Connecticut, Maine, Massachusetts, Rhode Island, and Vermont; however, the awarded funds are only included in the funding total for Massachusetts.

[b] In February 2011, Florida Governor Rick Scott returned the state's $1 million exchange planning grant.

[c] In August 2011, Kansas Governor Sam Brownback returned the state's $31.5 million early innovator grant.

[d] Louisiana's $998,416 exchange planning grant was returned in March 2011.

[e] A New Hampshire bill (HB 601) that became law in July 2011 instructed the state insurance commissioner to return $666,000 in exchange planning grant funds.

[f] Oklahoma's $54 million early innovator grant was returned in April 2011.

[g] In January 2012, Wisconsin Governor Scott Walker returned the state's $37.7 million early innovator grant.

End Notes

[1] ACA was signed into law on March 23, 2010 (P.L. 111-148, 124 Stat. 119). A week later, on March 30, 2010, the President signed the Health Care and Education Reconciliation Act (HCERA; P.L. 111-152, 124 Stat. 1029), which amended multiple health care and revenue provisions in ACA. Several other bills that were subsequently enacted during the 111th and 112th Congresses made more targeted changes to specific ACA provisions. All references to ACA in this report refer to the law as amended.

[2] For more detailed information about exchanges, see CRS Report R42663, Health Insurance Exchanges Under the Patient Protection and Affordable Care Act (ACA), by Bernadette Fernandez and Annie L. Mach.

[3] §§ 1311(b) and 1321(c) of P.L. 111-148.

[4] Alaska is the only state that did not apply for a planning grant.

[5] Center for Consumer Information and Insurance Oversight (CCIIO), April 8, 2013, at http://cciio.cms.gov/Archive/ Grants/exchanges-map.html.

[6] Authors' calculation based on data found in Table 3.

[7] HHS press release, February 16, 2011, at http://www.hhs.gov/news/press/2011pres/02/ 20110216a.html.

[8] http://cciio.cms.gov/.

In: States' Establishment of Health Insurance ... ISBN: 978-1-62808-575-4
Editors: F. C. Lewis and E. O. Walker

Chapter 3

HEALTH INSURANCE EXCHANGES UNDER THE PATIENT PROTECTION AND AFFORDABLE CARE ACT (ACA)*

Bernadette Fernandez and Annie L. Mach

SUMMARY

The fundamental purpose of a health insurance exchange is to provide a structured marketplace for the sale and purchase of health insurance. The authority and responsibilities of an exchange may vary, depending on statutory or other requirements for its establishment and structure. The Patient Protection and Affordable Care Act (ACA, P.L. 111-148, as amended) requires health insurance exchanges to be established in every state by January 1, 2014. ACA provides certain requirements for the establishment of exchanges, while leaving other choices to be made by the states.

Qualified individuals and small businesses will be able to purchase private health insurance through exchanges. Issuers selling health insurance plans through an exchange will have to follow certain rules, such as meeting the private market reform requirements in ACA. While the fundamental purpose of the exchanges will be to facilitate the offer and purchase of health insurance, nothing in the law prohibits qualified

* This is an edited, reformatted and augmented version of a Congressional Research Service publication, CRS Report for Congress R42663, from www.crs.gov, prepared for Members and Committees of Congress, dated January 31, 2013.

individuals, qualified employers, and insurance carriers from participating in the health insurance market outside of exchanges. Moreover, ACA explicitly states that enrollment in exchanges is voluntary and no individual may be compelled to enroll in exchange coverage.

Exchanges may be established either by the state itself as a "state exchange" or by the Secretary of Health and Human Services (HHS) as a "federally-facilitated exchange." A federally-facilitated exchange may be operated solely by the federal government, or it may be operated by the federal government in conjunction with the state, as a "partnership" exchange. All exchanges are required to carry out many of the same functions and adhere to many of the same standards, although there are important differences between the types of exchanges. States had to declare their intentions to establish their own exchange no later than December 14, 2012; to date, 17 states and D.C. have received conditional approval from HHS to operate a state exchange. States interested in pursuing a partnership exchange must declare their intentions no later than February 15, 2013.

ACA and regulations require exchanges to carry out a number of different functions. The primary functions relate to determining eligibility and enrolling individuals in appropriate plans, plan management, consumer assistance and accountability, and financial management. ACA gives various federal agencies, primarily HHS, responsibilities relating to the general operation of exchanges. Federal agencies are generally responsible for promulgating regulations, creating criteria and systems, and awarding grants to states to help them create and implement exchanges.

A state that is approved to operate its own exchange has a number of operational decisions to make, including decisions related to organizational structure (governmental agency or a nonprofit entity); types of exchanges (separate individual and Small Business Health Options Program (SHOP) exchanges, or a merged exchange); collaboration (a state may independently operate an exchange or enter into contracts with other states); service area (a state may establish one or more subsidiary exchanges in the state if each exchange serves a geographically distinct area and meets certain size requirements); contracted services (an exchange may contract with certain entities to carry out one or more responsibilities of the exchange); and governance (governing board and standards of conduct).

In general, health plans offered through exchanges will provide comprehensive coverage and meet all applicable private market reforms specified in ACA. Most exchange plans will provide coverage for "essential health benefits," at minimum; be subject to certain limits on cost-sharing, including out-of-pocket costs; and meet one of four levels of plan generosity based on actuarial value. To make exchange coverage more affordable, certain individuals will receive premium assistance in the form of federal tax credits. Moreover, some recipients of premium credits may also receive subsidies toward cost-sharing expenses.

This report outlines the required minimum functions of exchanges, and explains how exchanges are expected to be established and administered under ACA. The coverage offered through exchanges is discussed, and the report concludes with a discussion of how exchanges will interact with selected other ACA provisions.

INTRODUCTION

A health insurance exchange is a structured marketplace for the sale and purchase of health insurance. "Customers" can include individuals and businesses. The insurance companies ("issuers") that choose to sell their products through an exchange may be required to comply with consumer protections, such as offering insurance to every qualified applicant. Exchanges, however, are not issuers; rather, exchanges contract with issuers who will make insurance products available for purchase through exchanges. Essentially, exchanges are designed to bring together buyers and sellers of insurance, with the goal of increasing access to coverage.

This rather broad definition allows for a great deal of latitude, and therefore variance, in the number and scope of responsibilities covered in a particular exchange. For example, the role of an exchange may be more or less administrative: facilitating the sale and purchase of health insurance. An administrative-only exchange may function similar to websites that allow individuals to find airline travel options and purchase tickets (e.g., Kayak). Such an approach does not necessarily change or establish standards for the products being sold (whether they are health plans or airline tickets), or limit the types of buyers and sellers participating in the exchange, beyond what already exists in the private market. An example of a minimalist health insurance exchange is the Utah Health Exchange. Essentially, Utah's exchange is an Internet portal that is "designed to connect consumers to the information they need to make informed health care choices, and in the case of health insurance, to execute that choice electronically."[1]

At the other end of the spectrum, an exchange may have multiple functions beyond the role of insurance marketplace. For instance, an exchange may be responsible for implementing regulatory standards, such as requiring standardization of all products offered through it or imposing requirements on exchange participants. An exchange may be responsible for determining eligibility for exchange plans and government-provided subsidies.

An example of a more regulatory-oriented exchange is the Health Connector ("Connector") in Massachusetts. Similar to Utah's exchange, the Connector provides an online tool to allow consumers and others to find commercial health insurance options available to them. In addition, the Connector also manages a publicly subsidized coverage program for low-income state residents, and offers certificates to exempt individuals from the state's individual mandate, among other duties.[2]

An exchange may occupy a physical location and/or be virtual (i.e., performing its functions on the Internet). It may be governed by a public agency, a private entity, or a hybrid organization.

The insurance options offered through an exchange may also vary across insurance markets[3] and plan types. Nonetheless, while the authority and responsibilities of an exchange may vary, its fundamental purpose is to provide a venue where insurance companies may sell their insurance products and purchasers can compare and choose from multiple options available to them. Thus an exchange allows for "one-stop shopping" with respect to health insurance.

The exchange concept was included in the Patient Protection and Affordable Care Act (ACA, P.L. 111-148, as amended), as a means to increase access to health insurance. While ACA places many restrictions on the design and function of exchanges, the law also leaves many operational decisions to the states. Such flexibility will likely lead to variation in exchange models across the states.

For example, a state may decide to operate an exchange by itself, establish an exchange in partnership with the federal government, or leave this work entirely to the federal government.

States had to declare whether they will have a state exchange by December 14, 2012. By February 15, 2013, states must declare whether they will operate an exchange in partnership with the federal government. The initial open enrollment period for all exchanges will begin on October 1, 2013, and all exchanges are to be operational and offering coverage on January 1, 2014.

This report looks at the requirements for exchanges established in ACA and provides information on the requirements and choices available to states for the establishment, functions, financial responsibilities, and coverage of the ACA exchanges. It also includes a brief discussion of the interactions between exchanges and other provisions in the law.

ACA Exchanges

ACA intends exchanges to be marketplaces where qualified individuals and small businesses can "shop" for private health insurance coverage.[4] The coverage offered through exchanges will be comprehensive[5] and meet all applicable private market reforms[6] specified in ACA. Such plans offered through the exchanges will be certified as "qualified health plans" or QHPs.[7]

ACA explicitly states that enrollment in exchanges is voluntary and no individual may be compelled to enroll in exchange coverage.[8] While the main purpose of the exchanges will be to facilitate the offer and purchase of health insurance, nothing in the ACA prohibits qualified individuals, qualified small businesses, and insurance carriers from participating in the health insurance market outside of exchanges.[9]

For individuals seeking coverage, exchanges will not only create marketplaces where qualified individuals can purchase QHPs in the nongroup (individual) market, but exchanges will also assist individuals with obtaining federally subsidized premium and cost-sharing assistance to help low to middle income individuals offset the cost of both purchasing and using health insurance. Exchanges will also screen individuals for eligibility for certain public insurance programs (e.g., Medicaid) and connect them with appropriate agencies.

Small businesses seeking coverage for their employees will be able to use the small business health options program (SHOP) exchange. The SHOP exchange is designed to assist qualified small employers and their employees with the purchase of QHPs offered in the small group market. Qualified small employers will be able to select QHPs available in the SHOP to offer to their employees, and they will be able to set the amount they will contribute to QHP premiums.

ACA requires exchanges to be established in every state by January 1, 2014. Exchanges must be established by the state itself or by the Secretary of HHS,[10] and they must carry out the general functions described above for both individuals and small businesses. Additionally, exchanges will be expected to perform a number of other functions relating to managing the QHPs offered through the exchanges and assisting individuals and small businesses in accessing and obtaining coverage.

ESTABLISHMENT OF ACA EXCHANGES

ACA provides general direction regarding the establishment and administration of an exchange. ACA is supplemented by the final regulation on the establishment of exchanges and other guidance produced by federal agencies, particularly HHS.[11] Taken together, these documents set forth some requirements and minimum standards that various stakeholders—including consumers, states, issuers, and employers—must meet to be part of or to participate in an exchange.

One factor that could influence a number of determinations related to how an exchange is implemented is whether the exchange is established by a state or HHS. States have the option of establishing their own exchanges ("state exchange") as a governmental agency or a non-profit entity. If a state wants to operate its own exchange beginning January 1, 2014, it had to submit a "Declaration Letter" and an "Exchange Blueprint" application[12] to HHS by December 14, 2012. Eighteen states and D.C. submitted letters and applications prior to the deadline; to date, HHS has conditionally approved applications from 17 states and D.C.[13]

If a state's exchange is not approved, or if a state chooses not to establish its own exchange, the HHS Secretary has the authority to establish and operate an exchange in that state directly, or through an agreement with a non-profit entity.[14] In a "federally-facilitated exchange," HHS will carry out all functions of the exchange and have authority over the exchange. HHS gives states the option to enter into a hybrid type of exchange—somewhere between a state exchange and a federally-facilitated exchange. This option is referred to as a "partnership" with a federally-facilitated exchange, whereby certain state-designed and operated functions are combined with federally designed and operated functions. While HHS and states share responsibility for carrying out functions in partnerships within federally-facilitated exchanges, HHS retains authority over these exchanges.[15] If a state wants to have a partnership exchange, it must submit to HHS a Declaration Letter and an Exchange Blueprint application by February 15, 2013.

Regardless of whether an exchange is established by a state or the federal government, the initial open enrollment period for an exchange will be October 1, 2013, through March 31, 2014. Exchanges must begin offering coverage to qualified individuals and small businesses on January 1, 2014.[16]

State Exchanges

The HHS Secretary must approve the operation of a state exchange if it meets the following standards:

- the exchange is able to carry out the required functions of the exchange as established in the law and regulation, which include making QHPs available to qualified individuals and qualified employers;
- the exchange is capable of carrying out the information reporting requirements related to sharing information with the federal government in order to determine an individual's eligibility for a premium tax credit;[17] and
- either the entire geographic area of the state is covered in the exchange or the state has established multiple exchanges that cover the entire geographic area of the state.[18]

A state exchange is responsible for creating and implementing its structure and governing system according to the guidelines outlined in the statute and regulations, as discussed below.

Operational Structure of a State Exchange

A state that is approved to establish its own exchange has a number of decisions to make regarding the exchange's operational structure. A state must determine whether its exchange will be a governmental agency or a non-profit established by the state. The terms "governmental" and "non-profit established by the state" have not been defined; instead, it seems these terms are subject to state interpretation.[19]

A state can choose to independently operate an exchange, or a state can enter into contracts with other states (regardless of whether the states are contiguous) to operate a regional exchange.[20] States can also establish one or more subsidiary exchanges in the state if each exchange serves a geographically distinct area and if the area served by each exchange meets the geographic size requirement established in the law.[21] In other words, while states have a great deal of leeway in establishing how the exchange is divided up geographically, they must serve the entire population in their state. Furthermore, regional exchanges and subsidiary exchanges must meet all exchange requirements.

A state exchange must operate both the individual and SHOP exchanges, but a state can either merge the exchanges and operate both under the same administrative and governance structures, or elect to create separate administrative and governance structures for the individual and SHOP exchanges.[22] Additionally, regional and subsidiary exchanges must perform the functions of a SHOP exchange. If an exchange chooses to operate an individual exchange and a SHOP exchange under two different governance and administrative structures, a SHOP exchange must cover the same geographic area as the regional or subsidiary individual exchange.[23]

States also have the authority to allow a state exchange to contract with the entities described below to carry out one or more responsibilities of the exchange.[24] States can grant this authority to state exchanges independent of whether an exchange is a governmental agency or a non-profit established by the state. For example, a state exchange that is a non-profit established by the state could contract with a state agency that meets the criteria below to carry out certain consumer assistance functions for the exchange.

A state exchange may contract with

- an entity, including a state agency other than a Medicaid agency, incorporated under and subject to the laws of at least one state, that has demonstrated experience on a state or regional basis in the individual and small group health insurance markets and in benefits coverage, but is not an issuer; and/or
- a state Medicaid agency.

Governance of a State Exchange

Generally, a state exchange must have a governing board that meets certain requirements; the board must[25]

- be administered under a publicly adopted operating charter or by-laws;
- hold regular meetings that are open to the public and announced in advance;
- ensure that the board's membership includes at least one voting member who is a consumer representative and is not made up of a majority of voting representatives with conflicts of interest (e.g., representatives of issuers); and

- ensure that a majority of the voting members on its governing board have relevant experience in the health care field (e.g., in health benefits administration, or in public health).

In addition, a state exchange is required to have in place and make publicly available a set of governance principles that include ethics, conflict of interest standards, transparency and accounting standards, and standards related to disclosure of financial interests. A state exchange must also implement procedures as to how members of the governing board will disclose any financial interests. The state exchange's governance principles are subject to periodic review by HHS.[26]

Federally-Facilitated Exchange

If a state chooses not to operate its own exchange or if a state does not have approval to operate its own exchange, the HHS Secretary is required to establish a "federally-facilitated exchange" in the state.[27] A federally-facilitated exchange can be implemented by HHS alone, or a state can enter into a "partnership" with a federally-facilitated exchange, combining state-designed and operated functions with federally designed and operated functions.[28] Partnerships are considered a subset of federally-facilitated exchanges, indicating that HHS has authority over partnerships in federally-facilitated exchanges.[29] States interested in pursuing a partnership exchange effective in 2014 must submit to HHS a Declaration Letter and an Exchange Blueprint application by February 15, 2013.[30]

The final rule on the establishment of exchanges does not include provisions specific to federally-facilitated exchanges (instead saying that information for these exchanges will be provided in future guidance). However, the final rule does indicate that federally-facilitated exchanges are required to carry out many of the same functions as state exchanges. Additionally, federally-facilitated exchanges and state exchanges must adhere to many of the same standards outlined in ACA and the final rule. For example, state exchanges and federally-facilitated exchanges are both required to offer the same tools to help consumers access an exchange and assess their plan options through an exchange.

HHS has published some guidance that generally describes how a non-partnership federally-facilitated exchange will operate within the framework established by ACA and the final rule.[31] A detailed analysis of the guidance is beyond the scope of this report; however, the guidance generally describes how a non-partnership federally-facilitated exchange will determine which plans will be offered through an exchange, how it will conduct eligibility and enrollment activities, and how it will operate the SHOP exchange. The guidance also indicates that further guidance on non-partnership federally-facilitated exchanges is forthcoming.

With regard to the partnership exchange, HHS retains authority over the exchange, but it expects states to assume responsibility for certain exchange activities.[32] To enter into a partnership exchange, a state must either manage activities related to plan management or consumer assistance or both. If a state elects to administer plan management activities, the state will be responsible for recommending plans for certification to be offered through an exchange and managing day-to-day administration and oversight of exchange plans. If a state elects to perform consumer assistance activities in a partnership exchange, then the state will be responsible for providing in-person assistance to individuals applying for or enrolled in coverage offered through the exchange and can choose to be responsible for outreach and educational activities. If a state elects to administer both the plan management and consumer assistance activities within the partnership, then the state will carry out all of the activities described above.[33]

WHAT EXCHANGES DO

Exchanges are required to carry out a number of different functions, including determining eligibility and enrolling individuals in appropriate plans; conducting plan management activities; assisting consumers; ensuring plan accountability; and providing financial management.[34]

These functions are not necessarily exhaustive of exchange responsibilities; rather, this section is intended to provide a general overview of an exchange's responsibilities. Unless otherwise noted, both state and federally-facilitated exchanges are required to carry out the functions described in this section. Additionally, some responsibilities may be different for individual exchanges and SHOP exchanges, so the following discussion provides information for both.

Eligibility and Enrollment

Exchanges are responsible for a variety of functions related to determining an applicant's eligibility (whether an individual's or an employer's) for various plans/programs and for enrolling eligible applicants into those plans/programs. Exchanges must verify the information received from applicants and re-determine eligibility as necessary. Exchanges are expected to have secure electronic databases in place that support exchanges' eligibility and enrollment responsibilities by allowing information to be shared among state and federal agencies.[35] An exchange's responsibilities to determine eligibility and to enroll eligible individuals are different, but related, for the individual exchange and the SHOP exchange (for small business employees).

Flexibility Related to Eligibility and Enrollment Systems

ACA intends to create a seamless eligibility and enrollment system for individuals seeking health insurance coverage in the nongroup market and/or through public programs (e.g., Medicaid). The system would allow individuals to fill out a single application that collects the information necessary to screen the individual for multiple types of coverage and financial assistance. The system would then facilitate the enrollment of the individual in the appropriate plan/program.

States have some flexibility in designing and implementing this streamlined system. The flexibility is related to how eligibility and enrollment responsibilities will be shared among entities, including individual exchanges. ACA requires that the system is able to determine an applicant's eligibility for enrollment in a QHP[36] and for insurance affordability programs (IAP),[37] which include Medicaid, the State Children's Health Insurance Program (CHIP), the Basic Health Program (BHP),[38] advanced payment of premium tax credits, and cost-sharing reductions.

ACA and regulations allow different entities to participate in the eligibility and enrollment system. For example, the system can be designed to enable one entity (e.g., the individual exchange) to determine eligibility for and effectuate enrollment in QHPs and all IAPs.

Alternatively, the system can be designed so that one state agency determines eligibility for one IAP (i.e., the state's Medicaid agency determines Medicaid eligibility) while another entity or other entities determine eligibility for other plans/programs.

Descriptions of the potential variations in eligibility and enrollment systems that may occur as a result of this flexibility are beyond the scope of this report. However, it is important to note that this section generally describes how an individual exchange would handle its eligibility and enrollment functions *if it were to carry out the functions*. The summaries of eligibility requirements for enrollment in plans/programs described in *Table 1*, *Table 2, Table 3*, and *Table 4* are the same regardless of which entity determines eligibility.

Individual Exchange

To determine eligibility, an individual exchange must use a single, streamlined application to collect information from an applicant and verify that information according to procedures identified in regulation. For example, an individual exchange is expected to verify an applicant's social security number by transmitting the number to HHS, which will consult the Social Security Administration and the Department of Homeland Security, as needed, to verify the number.[39]

An individual exchange is expected to re-determine an enrollee's eligibility if the individual exchange receives and verifies new information relating to the enrollee.

This information can come from the enrollee, as enrollees are required to report any change with respect to eligibility standards within 30 days of the change, or it can come from information the individual exchange finds through its required periodic examination of available information that might affect eligibility (e.g., whether an enrollee has died). An individual exchange is also expected to redetermine or re-assess the eligibility of all enrollees on an annual basis. However, re-determinations and re-assessments due to changes in status do not fully satisfy the requirement for annual re-determinations and re-assessments.[40]

Eligibility for Enrollment in a QHP

An individual exchange is required to *determine* an applicant's eligibility for enrollment in a QHP. If an applicant is determined eligible for a QHP, the individual exchange is expected to facilitate the applicant's enrollment into the QHP selected by the individual. *Table 1* shows the criteria an individual exchange must use to determine eligibility for enrollment in a QHP.

Table 1. Criteria for Determining Eligibility for Enrollment in a QHP

An individual exchange must determine an applicant eligible for a QHP if the applicant meets the following criteria:	
Enrollment in a QHP	• Citizen, national, or noncitizen who is lawfully present in the United States[a]
	• Not incarcerated, other than pending the disposition of charges
	• Meets applicable state residency standards

Source: CRS analysis of ACA (as amended) and 77 Federal Register 18310, March 27, 2012.

[a] Only lawful residents may obtain exchange coverage; unauthorized aliens will be prohibited from obtaining coverage through an exchange, even if they could pay the entire premium without a subsidy.

Eligibility for Premium Tax Credits and Cost-Sharing Subsidies

Certain individuals who purchase a QHP through an individual exchange will be eligible for financial assistance to help them off-set the cost of the coverage and to defray some costs associated with using health services. ACA provides assistance, for the purchase of exchange coverage, in the form of premium tax credits. (A tax credit is a reduction that is applied to the amount an individual (or family) owes, if any, when filing income taxes.) Premium tax credits are advanceable, meaning instead of having to wait until after the end of the tax year to receive the credit, the individual may receive the payments in advance to coincide with when insurance premiums are due (usually on a monthly basis).

In addition to the premium tax credits, ACA provides cost-sharing subsides to certain individuals to help them pay costs related to the use of health services. (Cost-sharing generally refers to costs that an individual must pay when using services that are covered under the health plan that the person is enrolled in; common forms of cost-sharing include copayments and deductibles.) Both premium tax credits and cost-sharing subsidies are discussed later in this report under the section "Cost Assistance."

Because the premium tax credits are advanceable, it will be necessary to determine an individual's eligibility for the credits at the time the individual applies for coverage through an exchange. In regard to advanced payment of premium tax credits, an individual exchange may either *determine* an applicant's eligibility directly or *implement a determination* of eligibility made by HHS.[41] Determining eligibility directly is similar to determining eligibility for QHPs; the individual exchange reviews an applicant's information and makes a determination of eligibility. If an individual exchange chooses to determine an applicant's eligibility for advance payment of premium tax credits, the exchange must calculate the amount of the advance payment in accordance with Section 36B of the Internal Revenue Code. An individual exchange may only provide the advance payment if the applicant meets the eligibility criteria (see *Table 2).*

Similarly, an individual exchange may either directly determine eligibility for cost-sharing subsidies, or it may implement a determination made by HHS. If an individual exchange chooses to determine an applicant's eligibility for cost-sharing subsidies, the exchange must do so according to the criteria outlined in *Table 2.*

If an individual exchange decides *not* to directly determine eligibility for advanced payment of premium tax credits or *not* to directly determine eligibility for cost-sharing subsidies but rather implements HHS determinations, then an individual exchange is expected to transmit all collected and verified information to HHS. The individual exchange does not make a recommendation in this process; rather, the individual exchange shares information with HHS and then is expected to adhere to the determination of eligibility made by HHS.[42]

Eligibility for Medicaid and CHIP

An individual exchange may either *determine* or *assess* an applicant's eligibility for enrollment in Medicaid and/or CHIP. If an individual exchange *determines* eligibility for Medicaid and/or CHIP, then the individual exchange is also responsible for the enrollment of eligible applicants.

Once an applicant has been determined eligible, the individual exchange must transmit the applicant's information to the state Medicaid or CHIP agency, thus effectuating enrollment.

An individual exchange may only *assess* eligibility for Medicaid/CHIP. If an applicant is assessed eligible for a program the individual exchange is required to transmit all collected and verified information to the state Medicaid or CHIP agency to enable the agency to make a final determination of the applicant's eligibility. In this case, the exchange is only making a recommendation and sharing information with the appropriate agency; it is not responsible for making a final determination of eligibility. The individual exchange is expected to adhere to the final determination made by the agency.

Table 2. Criteria for Determining Eligibility for Subsidies Through an Exchange

An exchange or HHS may determine an applicant eligible for the subsidies below according to the following criteria:	
Advanced payment of premium tax credits	• Meets the criteria for eligibility for enrollment in a QHP through an exchange[a]
	• Not eligible for minimum essential coverage[b] other than • through the individual health insurance market; or • employer-sponsored insurance that is "unaffordable" or does not provide "minimum value"[c]
	• Is part of a tax-filing unit
	• Is enrolled in a QHP offered through an exchange
	• Has household income that either • is between 100% and 400% FPL; or • is not greater than 100% FPL and is an alien lawfully present (but not eligible for Medicaid because of duration of U.S. residency)[d]
Cost-sharing subsidies[e]	• Meets the criteria for eligibility for advance payment of premium tax credits
	• Is enrolled in a silver plan through an exchange[f]
	• Meets the criteria for eligibility for enrollment in a QHP through an exchangeHas household income between 100% and 400% FPL[g]

Source: CRS analysis of ACA (as amended) and 77 Federal Register 18310, March 27, 2012.

[a] These criteria are detailed in Table 1.

[b] The definition of minimum essential coverage is discussed in CRS Report R41331, Individual Mandate and Related Information Requirements under ACA, by Janemarie Mulvey and Hinda Chaikind.

[c] For the purpose of this provision, ACA considers an employer-sponsored plan "unaffordable" if the employee's premium contribution to the employer's self-only plan exceeds 9.5% of household income. An employer-sponsored plan does not provide "minimum value" if it covers less than 60% of total allowed costs (on average).

[d] The Personal Responsibility and Work Opportunity Reconciliation Act of 1996 (P.L. 104-193) determined that most individuals who are not citizens but are lawfully present in the United States are barred from Medicaid for the first five years that they are in the United States.

[e] ACA establishes different eligibility criteria for cost-sharing subsidies for certain American Indians and Alaska Natives. For more information, see CRS Report R41152, Indian Health Care: Impact of the Affordable Care Act (ACA), by Elayne J. Heisler.

[f] A description of the different tiers of coverage offered through an exchange is included in the "Coverage Levels and Benefits" section of this report.

[g] The cost-sharing subsidies reduce the annual caps on out-of-pocket expenses for individuals with income between 100% and 400% FPL. Additionally, ACA requires QHP issuers to further reduce cost-sharing requirements for individuals with income between 100% and 250% FPL. For more information, see CRS Report R41137, Health Insurance Premium Credits in the Patient Protection and Affordable Care Act (ACA), by Bernadette Fernandez and Thomas Gabe.

The final rule on Medicaid eligibility changes under ACA indicates that the state Medicaid and/or CHIP agency will decide whether an individual exchange will determine or assess eligibility for its program(s).[43] Additionally, the rule clarifies that some individuals have financial eligibility for Medicaid based on modified adjusted gross income (MAGI), while others do not have financial eligibility based on MAGI.[44] The rule provides that a state's Medicaid agency can separately decide on the individual exchange's role in determining or assessing Medicaid eligibility for MAGI and non-MAGI populations. *Table 3* shows criteria an individual exchange must use to determine or assess eligibility for individuals whose financial eligibility is based on MAGI. It is beyond the scope of this report to detail the criteria used to determine or assess eligibility for individuals whose financial eligibility is not based on MAGI.

Eligibility for Enrollment in a BHP

The Basic Health Program (BHP) is a health insurance program for low-income individuals who are not eligible for Medicaid, and is offered in lieu of eligible individuals obtaining coverage through an exchange. States have the option to implement the BHP, and therefore, exchanges will interact with BHPs in only those states that choose to implement a BHP.

If a state chooses to establish a BHP, an individual exchange is expected to *determine* an applicant's eligibility for a BHP, and facilitate the applicant's enrollment in the program. *Table 4* shows the criteria an individual exchange must use to determine eligibility for enrollment in a BHP.

Table 3. Criteria for Determining or Assessing MAGI-Based Eligibility for Enrollment in Medicaid and CHIP

An individual exchange may determine an applicant eligible or assess an applicant's eligibility for MAGI- based Medicaid and CHIP according to the following criteria:		
	Determination	Assessment
Enrollment in Medicaid	• Meets the non-financial criteria for Medicaid for populations whose eligibility is based on modified adjusted gross income (MAGI)[a] • Has a household income that is at or below the applicable Medicaid MAGI-based income standard • Is either a pregnant woman, under age 19, a parent or caretaker of a dependent child, or is under age 65 and not entitled to or enrolled in Medicare Parts A or B	• Makes the assessment based on the applicable Medicaid MAGI-based income standards and citizenship and immigration status, using verification rules and procedures consistent with Medicaid statute, regardless of how such standards are implemented by the state Medicaid agency • Must adhere to state Medicaid agency's final determination of applicant's eligibility
Enrollment in CHIP	• Meets the requirements for children to enroll in CHIP[b] • Has a household income at or below the applicable CHIP MAGI-based income standard	• Makes the assessment based on the applicable CHIP MAGI-based income standards and citizenship and immigration status, using verification rules and procedures consistent with CHIP statute, regardless of how such standards are implemented by the state CHIP agency • Must adhere to state CHIP agency's final determination of applicant's eligibility

Source: CRS analysis of ACA (as amended) and 77 Federal Register 18310, March 27, 2012.

[a] For information about populations whose Medicaid eligibility is, in part, based on MAGI-based income, see CRS Report R41210, Medicaid and the State Children's Health Insurance Program (CHIP) Provisions in ACA: Summary and Timeline, by Evelyne P. Baumrucker et al.

[b] For more information about children's eligibility for CHIP, see CRS Report R40444, State Children's Health Insurance Program (CHIP): A Brief Overview, by Elicia J. Herz and Evelyne P. Baumrucker.

Table 4. Criteria for Determining Eligibility for Enrollment in a BHP

An individual exchange must determine an applicant eligible for a BHP if the applicant meets the following criteria:	
Enrollment in the Basic Health Program (BHP)	• Resident of a state and not eligible for the state's Medicaid program • Not eligible for minimum essential coverage or is eligible for employer-sponsored insurance (ESI) that is not affordable[a] • Has not attained age 65 at the beginning of the plan year • Has household income that either • exceeds 133% of the federal poverty level (FPL) but does not exceed 200% FPL; or • is not greater than 133% FPL and is an alien lawfully present (but not eligible for Medicaid because of duration of U.S. residency)[b]

Source: CRS analysis of ACA (as amended) and 77 Federal Register 18310, March 27, 2012.

[a] The definition of minimum essential coverage is discussed in CRS Report R41331, Individual Mandate and Related Information Requirements under ACA, by Janemarie Mulvey and Hinda Chaikind. ACA considers employer coverage "unaffordable" if the employee's contribution toward the employer's lowest-cost self-only premium exceeds 9.5% of household income.

[b] The Personal Responsibility and Work Opportunity Reconciliation Act of 1996 (P.L. 104-193) determined that most individuals who are not citizens but are lawfully present in the United States are barred from Medicaid for the first five years that they are in the United States.

SHOP Exchange

As the exchange for small businesses, the SHOP has responsibilities similar to the individual exchange in that the SHOP is also responsible for collecting and verifying information from employers and employees (both considered applicants), determining eligibility, and facilitating enrollment. An employer and each of its employees seeking coverage must submit an application to the SHOP. The SHOP must process the applications, and if the employer and employees are determined eligible, the SHOP must facilitate the enrollment of qualified employees into QHPs offered through the SHOP.

A qualified employee is an employee who receives an offer of coverage from a qualified employer. A qualified employer is a small group employer[45] that elects to make, at a minimum, all full-time employees eligible for one or more QHPs offered in the small group market through an exchange, and has its principal business in the exchange service area or offers coverage to each eligible employee through the SHOP serving the employee's worksite.[46]

The SHOP is required to verify applicants' eligibility as outlined in regulation.[47] The SHOP must permit an employer to purchase coverage for employees at any time during the year, but the employer's plan must consist of a 12-month period beginning with the employer's effective date of coverage. Employees must adhere to annual open enrollment periods as determined by the SHOP, with special allowances for newly qualified employees.

Employers are not required to offer all the plans in an exchange to their employees. The SHOP must allow an employer to limit the selection of plans.[48] An employer who uses the SHOP is not required to contribute to employees' premiums; additionally, neither ACA nor regulations specify whether a SHOP can require a minimum contribution from employers.[49]

Plan Management Responsibilities

Exchanges are required to ensure that QHPs are certified.[50] An exchange may certify a plan as a QHP if the plan meets the required minimum criteria and if the exchange determines that it is in the best interest of qualified individuals and employers to have such a plan available.[51]

The minimum certification criteria outlined in ACA and further defined through regulation include requirements related to marketing, choice of providers, plan networks, accreditation,[52] and other features.[53]

In addition to certifying QHPs, an exchange must establish processes for recertification and decertification of QHPs. The recertification process, at a minimum, must include a review of the general certification criteria and must be completed on or before September 15 of the applicable calendar year. The decertification process must, at a minimum, include the following requirements: the ability for an exchange to decertify a plan at any time if the exchange determines that the QHP no longer meets the certification requirements; an exchange must establish a process for the appeal of a decertification; and an exchange must provide a notice of the decertification to all affected parties, including the QHP issuer, the exchange enrollees, HHS, and the state insurance department.

An exchange has additional plan management functions. For example, the exchange must require plans seeking certification as QHPs to submit justification for premium increases before it takes effect, and the plans will have to post the information about their premium increases on their websites.[54]

Also, the HHS Secretary is required to create a system that rates QHPs on the basis of relative quality and price. An exchange is expected to assign a rating to each QHP according to the HHS Secretary's criteria and provide the quality rating information through its website.[55]

Consumer Assistance and Accountability

Exchanges have a number of responsibilities related to assisting consumers in accessing and obtaining coverage, including providing tools to help consumers access the exchange, helping consumers determine which plan or program to enroll in, and helping consumers determine their potential financial responsibility for a QHP offered through an exchange.[56] Additionally, exchanges are expected to adhere to accountability practices to increase an exchange's transparency.

The following are some of an exchange's responsibilities related to assisting consumers and being accountable to stakeholders, including consumers. An exchange must

- Provide for operation of a toll-free telephone hotline that addresses the needs of consumers requesting assistance and informs individuals with disabilities and limited English proficiency of the availability of services to assist them.
- Maintain a website which, among other things, provides standardized comparative information on each QHP available through the exchange and allows qualified individuals to select a QHP in which to enroll.[57]
- Make available an electronic calculator (through its website) that facilitates the comparison of available QHPs (including the impact of any advance payments of tax credits and cost-sharing subsidies in the

individual exchange and the impact of any employer contribution in the SHOP exchange).

- Conduct outreach and education activities that will educate consumers about the exchange and insurance affordability programs (IAPs) to encourage participation.[58]
- Establish a Navigator program with grants to eligible individuals and entities to provide information about the exchange and help individuals select a QHP. Navigators are also required to conduct activities to raise awareness of an exchange.[59]
- Include results on its website from the Secretary's survey on enrollee satisfaction with the QHPs offered through the exchange, in a manner that allows for easy comparisons of enrollee satisfaction levels.[60]
- Regularly consult with stakeholders regarding the accessibility and administration of an exchange. These stakeholders include enrollees of QHPs; individuals and entities with experience in facilitating enrollment in health insurance coverage; advocates for hard to reach populations (e.g., individuals with substance abuse problems); small businesses, large employers, and self-employed individuals; state Medicaid and CHIP agencies; federally recognized Tribes; public health experts; issuers; and health insurance agents and brokers.[61]
- Share financial information on its website, regarding: any regulatory fees or other payments required by the exchange; administrative costs of the exchange; and monies lost to waste, fraud, and abuse.[62]
- Determine the role of agents and brokers in the exchange. An exchange may allow agents and brokers to be Navigators, provided they otherwise meet the Navigator eligibility criteria.[63] An exchange may also allow agents and brokers to enroll individuals and employers in QHPs offered through an exchange if the agents and brokers meet certain requirements.[64]

Financial Management

Exchanges are responsible for financial management and are expected to be self-sustaining by 2015. They have been given authority to generate funding to support their operations; however, while the law and regulation describe this authority, neither specify how an exchange may or may not generate funding.[65] An example provided in regulation is that exchanges could charge participating issuers assessments or user fees.[66]

Exchanges are expected to play a role in collecting premiums and distributing the premiums to issuers. ACA requires exchanges to perform certain functions relating to financial oversight and integrity, including keeping an accurate accounting of all financial activities and submitting a report annually to the HHS Secretary concerning such accountings. Exchanges are also required to cooperate with investigations into the affairs of exchanges, conducted by the HHS Secretary in coordination with HHS Inspector General.[67]

ACA Risk Mitigation Programs

Exchanges are expected to deal with the potential for adverse selection. Adverse selection occurs when a large number of individuals who expect or plan for high use of health services enroll in more generous and often more expensive health plans (i.e., a woman who plans to become pregnant switches from a plan with less generous maternity benefits to a plan with more generous maternity benefits), while simultaneously individuals who expect or plan for low use of health services enroll in more modest plans, both in terms of price and benefits. Adverse selection can lead to health plans that have risk pools with a large number of high-cost individuals, which can lead to higher costs for individuals in the pool, and in extreme instances, possible dissolution of the pool due to an increasingly expensive risk pool.

ACA establishes three risk programs to help mitigate the potential impact of adverse selection: reinsurance, risk corridors, and risk adjustment. The first two programs are temporary and are intended to provide some protection against risk in the short term before a full risk adjustment program can be developed. None of the programs are specific to exchanges; rather, they are tools that can be used both inside and outside the exchanges to mitigate the impact of adverse selection. For more information about ACA's risk programs, see *a*

FEDERAL RESPONSIBILITIES FOR ESTABLISHMENT AND ADMINISTRATION OF ALL EXCHANGES

ACA requires federal agencies, primarily HHS, to oversee the exchanges, thus carrying out a number of responsibilities related to the establishment and administration of exchanges. Many of these responsibilities require federal agencies to create systems and criteria. For example, the HHS Secretary is required to develop the minimum criteria an exchange will use to certify QHPs to be offered through an exchange.[68] The HHS Secretary is also required to grant financial awards to states to be used to establish exchanges.

Federal Oversight

Federal agencies, primarily HHS, have oversight and other responsibilities for exchanges. These responsibilities not only relate to the general operation of the exchange, but they also relate to how an exchange is expected to share information and coordinate its duties with federal agencies.

It is beyond the scope of this report to detail all of the responsibilities ACA gives to federal agencies;[69] however, the following are general examples of duties required of federal agencies. Other examples are included in this report, where appropriate.

- The HHS Secretary is required to promulgate regulations relating to, among other things, setting standards for the establishment and operation of exchanges, the offering of QHPs through exchanges, and the establishment of the reinsurance and risk adjustment programs established by ACA.[70]
- The HHS Secretary is expected to coordinate efforts between the exchange and other federal agencies (such as the Social Security Administration) to verify information collected by the exchange from applicants and related to eligibility for the exchange and other programs (e.g., premium tax credits).[71]
- The HHS Secretary is expected, through consultation with other entities (such as the National Association of Insurance Commissioners), to develop and maintain tools and set minimum standards for tools that exchanges may use to assist consumers with accessing the exchange.[72]

Federal Financial Assistance

While exchanges are expected to be self-sufficient by 2015, there is some limited federal assistance provided to states to help them as they develop their exchanges.[73] ACA requires the HHS Secretary to award planning and establishment grants to states for the purposes of activities related to establishing exchanges.[74] ACA gives the HHS Secretary the authority to determine the amount of the grants and to renew the grants if a state is making sufficient progress toward establishing an exchange. No planning and establishment grant may be awarded after December 31, 2014.[75]

Planning grants were given to 49 states and the District of Columbia.[76] These grants of up to $1 million each were intended to provide resources to states to help them conduct research and planning related to establishing exchanges. Establishment grants have also been awarded to a number of states. Level one establishment grants are annual awards to states that are still in the initial phases of developing exchanges, and level two establishment grants are multi-year awards intended to assist states that have made significant progress in implementation of exchanges.

To date, 34 states and the District of Columbia have received level one grants, and 11 states and the District of Columbia have received level two grants.[77] In total, the states and the District of Columbia have received about $3.5 billion in establishment grants.[78]

The HHS Secretary is also required to award grants to eligible entities to help them develop and adapt technology systems to be used by an exchange to determine eligibility and process enrollment.[79] These "early innovator" grants were given to seven entities to help them design and implement the information technology infrastructure needed to operate an exchange.[80] The grants were awarded to entities that have "demonstrated their technical expertise and ability to develop these IT systems on a fast track schedule, and their willingness to share design and implementation solutions with other states."[81] The seven entities combined have received more than $249 million in early innovator grants.[82]

Coverage Offered through the Exchanges

Most private health insurance plans sold through exchanges must include a comprehensive set of benefits. The law specifies standards for the types and levels of coverage that can be offered through exchanges.

Coverage Levels and Benefits

Generally, exchange plans must (1) cover "essential health benefits" (EHBs), at a minimum; (2) limit cost-sharing, including out-of-pocket costs; and (3) provide coverage that meets one of four levels of plan generosity based on actuarial value (defined below).[83] These requirements will become effective beginning in 2014, to dovetail with the establishment of exchanges. The following discusses them in greater detail.

Essential Health Benefits

ACA does not explicitly list the benefits that comprise essential health benefits (EHBs). Instead, the law identifies 10 broad benefit categories which must be included in EHBs, at a minimum:

- ambulatory patient services;
- emergency services;
- hospitalization;
- maternity and newborn care;
- mental health and substance use disorder services, including behavioral health treatment;
- prescription drugs;
- rehabilitative and habilitative services and devices;
- laboratory services;
- preventive and wellness and chronic disease management; and
- pediatric services, including oral and vision care.

States may impose additional benefit mandates beyond what is required under EHBs. However, any state that requires health plans to offer benefits beyond EHBs must assume the total cost of providing those additional benefits, for all the plans, and regardless of whether or not an individual is receiving any financial assistance with premiums or cost-sharing. The state must make payments either directly to the individuals enrolled in health plans affected by the state benefit mandates, or to such plans on behalf of enrolled individuals.[84]

The bulk of the responsibility for defining EHBs is given to the HHS Secretary, who must then notify the public and provide the opportunity for comment. The HHS Secretary has certain guidelines that must be followed in developing the EHBs, including ensuring that the scope of EHBs is equal to the scope of benefits under a "typical" employer-provided health plan (as certified by the Chief Actuary of the Centers for Medicare & Medicaid Services), and that EHBs meet equity and other standards specified in the law. To assist the HHS Secretary in this determination, the law requires the Secretary of the Department of Labor (Labor) to conduct a survey of employer-provided health coverage.[85]

ACA did not specify a deadline for when the Secretary is required to define EHBs. As of the cover date of this report, HHS has not issued regulations defining EHBs; however, in a bulletin and in proposed rules, HHS indicated that the EHBs would be defined by a benchmark plan selected by each state.[86] HHS identified four benchmark plan types that a state could use for the purpose of defining EHBs in that state:

- one of the three largest plans in the state's small group health insurance market;[87]
- one of the three largest state employees health benefits plans;
- one of the three largest national plans offered through the Federal Employees Health Benefits Program (FEHBP); or
- the largest commercial non-Medicaid health maintenance organization in the state.

To assist states in this effort, HHS conducted studies that identified the largest plans (by enrollment) for several of the benchmark plan types listed above, and documented the prevalence of certain benefits in health plans that are currently offered.[88] HHS found that the largest national FEHBP plan, by far, is offered through Blue Cross and Blue Shield; and while small group plans vary by state, the ones with the largest enrollment generally are offered by large, commercial insurance carriers.

In general, HHS found that most of the EHB categories specified in ACA are consistently covered across different health plans and insurance markets, including benefits such as doctor visits, surgery, hospitalization, transplants, emergency department services, maternity care, mental health and substance abuse services, therapy, medical equipment, laboratory work, preventive care, and pediatric and child services. However, there are three EHB benefit categories that are excluded from many private health plans: pediatric oral care, pediatric vision care, and habilitative services. For these benefit categories, HHS proposes alternative approaches for supplementing benchmark plans that do not cover pediatric vision/oral care or habilitative services.[89]

HHS required states to specify a benchmark plan by December 26, 2012.[90] Each state's benchmark plan will apply to their respective exchanges for plan years 2014 and 2015. HHS will then revisit this issue for the 2016 plan year.[91] The default benchmark option, the largest plan by enrollment in the largest product in the state's small group market, will apply in cases where a state did not voluntarily select a benchmark plan.

Cost-Sharing Requirements

Cost-sharing includes deductibles and co-payments for services rendered. ACA limits the amount of cost-sharing that exchange plans generally may impose on enrolled individuals. These cost-sharing limits prohibit

- any deductible applicable to preventive health services;
- deductibles, in small group health plans, that are greater than $2,000 for self-only coverage, or $4,000 for any other coverage in 2014 (annually adjusted thereafter); and
- annual cost-sharing limits that exceed existing limits specified in the tax code, relating to certain high deductible health plans.[92]

Levels of Plan Generosity

Health plans that provide the essential health benefits package must tailor cost-sharing to meet one of four levels of generosity, based on actuarial value.[93] Actuarial value (AV) is a summary measure of a plan's generosity, expressed as the percentage of medical expenses estimated to be paid by the issuer for a standard population and set of allowed charges. In other words, AV reflects the relative share of cost-sharing that may be imposed. On average, the lower the AV, the greater the cost-sharing.[94]

Each level of plan generosity is designated according to a precious metal and corresponds to a specific actuarial value:

Levels	Actuarial Value
Bronze	60%
Silver	70%
Gold	80%
Platinum	90%

While the term actuarial value may imply a high level of precision,

> actuarial analysis is inherently an estimation process and hence is somewhat inexact. Actuarial value estimates will vary by the data

> sources, projection methods, and assumptions used, and there may be a reasonable range of appropriate methods and assumptions used to develop these estimates.[95]

Given this, ACA requires the HHS Secretary to promulgate regulations regarding the determination of the levels of plan generosity. The determination will be based on a benefit package consisting of essential health benefits and a standard population. To date, HHS issued a bulletin that described its proposed definition for actuarial value and solicited comments. In the bulletin, HHS proposes to use a standard data set based on a countrywide standard population, with the option for individual states to "develop State standard populations based on State claims data."[96]

Exchange Health Plans

Exchanges will offer several types of health plans, as specified in statute and regulation. Exchange plans will provide a comprehensive set of covered benefits (i.e., the essential health benefits), except for stand-alone dental plans (which will have to meet a narrow set of benefit requirements). While most of these comprehensive plans will be available to any individual or employer who is qualified to enroll in exchanges (such as multi-state QHPs and CO-OP QHPs),[97] some plans will be available only to specific subpopulations (child-only QHPs and catastrophic QHPs).[98] Finally, some plans offered in exchanges may also be offered outside of exchanges.[99]

Qualified Health Plans

In general, exchanges will offer comprehensive coverage that meets the standards to be certified as "qualified health plans" (QHPs),[100] provided it meets requirements related to marketing, choice of providers, plan networks, and other features, or is recognized by each exchange through which such plan is offered.[101] In addition, all QHPs are required to comply with benefit, cost-sharing, and generosity components of the essential health benefits package (described above). In addition to qualified health plans, exchanges will also offer multi-state QHPs, child-only QHPs, and COOP QHPs (described below).[102]

An issuer of QHPs must be licensed and in good standing with each state in which it offers coverage; must offer at least one QHP each providing silver and gold levels of coverage; and must comply with regulations applicable to exchanges. An issuer may offer QHPs outside of exchanges as well as inside, but the premiums would have to be the same, even if the QHP is sold through an insurance agent.[103]

Multi-State Plans

Multi-state plans (MSPs) are designed to offer nationally available QHPs, so that individuals and small businesses will all have access to these plans, regardless of where they live. The Director of the Office of Personnel Management (OPM) will enter into contracts with issuers to offer at least two MSPs ultimately through every exchange in all the states.[104] Any individual eligible to purchase insurance through the exchange may enroll in an MSP. Enrollment is voluntary, and individuals may be eligible for premium credits and cost-sharing assistance.

Each contract for an MSP will be for at least one year and can be automatically renewed if neither party provides notice to terminate. At least one contract will be with a nonprofit entity, and at least one contract cannot provide coverage for abortion services.[105] The OPM Director will enter into a contract with an issuer if the issuer offers the plan in at least 60% of states in the first year, at least 70% in the second year, at least 85% in the third year, and in all states thereafter.

An issuer offering a MSP must meet certain requirements and adhere to certain policies. For example, an issuer offering a MSP must meet the requirements in every state's exchange, offer a uniform benefits package in each state consisting of the essential health benefits, and comply with the minimum standards prescribed for carriers offering health benefits plans under the Federal Employees Health Benefits Program (FEHBP).[106] However, unlike other QHPs offered through an exchange, which are regulated by a state, MSPs will be licensed by states, but regulated by OPM. For example, OPM has the authority to certify, recertify, and decertify MSPs for participation in an exchange. If OPM certifies an MSP, the MSP is deemed certified to participate in every state's exchange.[107]

Child-Only Qualified Health Plans

ACA requires an issuer that offers a QHP through an exchange to also offer that plan as a "child-only plan."[108] Child-only plans will provide QHP coverage for individuals who are less than 21 years of age. The final regulation on exchanges stated that a child-only plan must be provided at the same level of coverage (bronze, silver, gold, or platinum) as a qualified health plan, as specified in the law.[109]

Consumer Operated and Oriented Plans

ACA establishes the Consumer Operated and Oriented Plan (CO-OP) program, with an intent to "foster the creation of qualified nonprofit health insurance issuers to offer qualified health plans in the individual and small group markets in the states in which the issuers are licensed to offer such plans."[110] ACA gives the HHS Secretary the authority to grant start-up and solvency loans to non-profit organizations applying to become qualified issuers.

Health plans offered by a CO-OP loan recipient may be deemed certified as a CO-OP QHP; if a plan is deemed a CO-OP QHP, then an exchange must recognize the plan as eligible to participate in an exchange.

CO-OP QHPs are eligible to participate in an exchange for two years and may be recertified every two years after that for up to 10 years following the life of any loan awarded. To be deemed certified, a CO-OP QHP must comply with the following: standards for certifying QHPs; all state-specific standards established by an exchange for QHPs operating in that state (except where those standards operate to exclude loan recipients due to being new issuers or based on characteristics that are inherent to being a CO-OP); and the standards of the CO-OP program as set forth in the law and the final rule relating to the CO-OP program.[111] CMS, or an entity designated by CMS, has the authority to deem CO-OP QHPs as certified to participate in an exchange.

CO-OP loan recipients must offer a CO-OP QHP at the silver and gold levels in every individual market exchange that serves the geographic regions in which the CO-OP loan recipient is licensed and intends to provide health care coverage. If offering at least one plan in the small group market, CO-OP loan recipients must offer a CO-OP QHP at both the silver and gold levels in each SHOP that serves the geographic regions in which the entity is offering coverage.

This indicates that CO-OP QHPs will be offered in at least the individual market in every exchange that shares a geographic region with a CO-OP loan recipient.[112] Individuals who enroll in CO-OP QHPs offered through the individual market are eligible for premium tax credits and cost-sharing subsidies.

The HHS Secretary began awarding CO-OP program loans in January 2012; as of December 21, 2012, 24 non-profits in 24 states had received loans.[113] On January 2, 2013, the American Taxpayer Relief Act of 2012 (P.L. 112-240) was enacted. The Act included a provision that rescinded nearly all unobligated funding for the CO-OP program. The only funding that was not rescinded was an amount set aside for governance and oversight of loans already awarded.[114]

Catastrophic Plan

Issuers may offer catastrophic plans in the exchanges,[115] which will have actuarial values less than what is required to meet any of the levels of plan generosity for qualified health plans (described above).

These plans are expected to have lower premiums, because they will have less generous coverage and higher cost-sharing. Catastrophic plans must

- be available only to individuals under 30 years of age, or individuals exempt from the individual mandate,[116] because they do not have access to affordable coverage or experienced a hardship;
- include coverage for "essential health benefits";
- include coverage for at least three primary care visits;
- have a deductible equal to existing cost-sharing limits specified in the tax code, relating to certain high deductible health plans[117] (the deductible will not apply to "preventive health services"); [118] and
- be offered only through the individual health insurance market.

Stand-Alone Dental Benefits

ACA allows issuers to offer stand-alone dental benefits through the exchanges, as long as such benefits include pediatric oral services (as specified under the essential health benefits provision).[119] The final exchange regulation clarifies that stand-alone dental benefits may be offered in a plan separate from a qualified health plan, or in conjunction with a QHP, as specified in the law. Exchanges may not limit the offer of stand-alone dental benefits to only one of these two options. In other words, issuers have sole discretion regarding (1) whether they will offer stand-alone dental benefits, and (2) the form in which those benefits will be provided (separate from or in conjunction with a QHP).

Cost Assistance

To make exchange coverage more affordable, certain individuals will receive premium assistance in the form of federal tax credits.[120] (As specified in the law, the Treasury Department will send monthly payments to the insurance company which issues the health plan in which a credit recipient is enrolled, to cover all or part of that person's monthly premium.)[121] Moreover, some recipients of premium credits may also receive subsidies towards cost-sharing expenses.[122] Exchanges have some responsibilities, as outlined below, in regard to determining an individual's eligibility for cost assistance and calculating the amount of cost assistance provided.

Premium Tax Credits

New federal tax credits were authorized in ACA to help low-middle income individuals pay for exchange coverage, beginning in 2014. The premium credit will be an advanceable, refundable tax credit, meaning tax filers need not wait until the end of the tax year in order to benefit from the credit (advance payments will actually go directly to the issuer),[123] and may claim the full credit amount even if they have little or no federal income tax liability.

To be eligible for a premium credit in an exchange, an individual must

- have household income[124] between 100% and 400% of the federal poverty level, with exceptions;[125]
- *not* be eligible "minimum essential coverage"[126] other than:
    - through the individual health insurance market; or
    - employer-sponsored insurance that is "unaffordable" or does not provide minimum value"; [127]
- be enrolled in an exchange plan; and
- be part of a tax-filing unit.

The amount of the tax credit will vary from person to person: it depends on the household income of the tax filer (and dependents), the premium for the exchange plan in which the tax filer (and dependents) is (are) enrolled, and other factors. In certain instances, the credit amount may cover the entire premium and the tax filer pays nothing towards the premium. In other instances, the tax filer may be required to pay part (or all) of the premium.[128]

Exchanges are responsible for either determining an individual's eligibility for advance payment of premium credits or implementing a determination made by HHS.[129] If an exchange makes the determination, then the exchange is also responsible for calculating the amount of the credit in accordance with Section 36B of the Internal Revenue Code.

Cost-Sharing Subsidies

Certain individuals who are eligible for premium credits in the exchanges will also be eligible for subsidies towards service-related cost-sharing.

(According to guidance issued by HHS, the federal government will provide monthly payments to the issuer of the health plan in which the subsidy recipient is enrolled, to reduce the amount of cost-sharing that individual would be responsible for when s/he uses health services.)[130] An individual who qualifies for the premium credit *and* is enrolled in a silver plan[131] through an exchange, will also be eligible for a cost-sharing subsidy. As discussed above, total cost-sharing in exchange plans will be limited according to amounts specified in the federal tax code.[132] Given that most exchange plans will already be required to meet such limits, the cost-sharing subsidies will further reduce the total amount those individuals who qualify for the subsidies will pay for using health services.[133]

Exchanges are required to either determine an individual's eligibility for cost-sharing subsidies or implement a determination made by HHS.[134] To do this, an exchange is expected to collect and verify the information necessary to make the determination and share that information with HHS.

INTERACTION WITH OTHER ACA PROVISIONS

Individual Mandate

Beginning in 2014, most individuals are required to have health insurance or potentially pay a penalty for noncompliance.[135] Generally, individuals will be required to maintain "minimum essential coverage" for themselves and their dependents.[136] Nearly all plans offered through exchanges qualify as minimum essential coverage. As follows, most individuals who have coverage through an exchange will meet the requirements of the individual mandate. Other coverage, such as employer-sponsored insurance and Medicaid, is also considered minimum essential coverage for the purpose of the individual mandate, so an individual does not have to enroll in an exchange plan to meet the requirements of the mandate.

Certain individuals will be exempt from the individual mandate. For example, some individuals will qualify for an exemption based on the affordability of coverage while others will qualify because of their religious beliefs. In screening applicants for eligibility for QHPs and IAPs, exchanges are required to determine whether an individual is exempt from the mandate and issue certificates of exemption accordingly.[137]

Employer Requirements

While employers are not required to offer health benefits to their employees, certain large employers may be subject to penalties whether or not they offer health insurance. Large employers who do *not* offer health insurance may be subject to penalties if any of their *full-time* workers enroll in exchange plans and receive premium credits. While most employers who *do* offer health benefits will meet the law's requirements, some also may be required to pay a penalty if any of their full-time workers receive a premium credit.[138]

In the latter scenario, one way that workers with an employer offer of health benefits may be eligible for premium credits is if the employer plan does not provide minimum value; that is, has an actuarial value that is less than 60%.[139] So while employers are not required to offer coverage through the exchanges, certain large employers may be subject to a penalty if they offer coverage with an actuarial value lower than a bronze-level plan and one of their full-time workers enrolls in an exchange and receives a premium credit.

Exchanges are responsible for notifying an employer if an employee has been found eligible for advance payment of premium credits or cost-sharing subsidies. The exchange must identify the employee, indicate the employee's eligibility, explain that the employer may be subject to penalty, and notify the employer of the right to appeal the determination.

Reforms to Private Health Insurance Markets

ACA includes a number of private market reforms that impose requirements on health insurance carriers and others. Such reforms relate to the offer, issuance, generosity, and pricing of health plans, among other requirements. For example, ACA requires most health plans to extend dependent coverage to children under age 26, with exception.[140] Given that health insurance carriers will be offering plans through the exchanges, ACA's private market reforms will apply to exchange plans.[141]

As discussed under the "Plan Management Responsibilities" section of this report, one of the responsibilities of exchanges will be to certify that plans meet the criteria for a qualified health plan, and, therefore, may be offered through an exchange. While the certification process will consider plan marketing requirements, provider network adequacy, and other features, as specified in the law, the market reforms are requirements imposed generally on insurance companies. Since states remain the primary regulators of health insurance, even post-ACA enactment, states would enforce ACA insurance requirements.

Medicaid

While Medicaid is generally beyond the scope of this report, ACA's Medicaid and exchange provisions were originally designed to work in tandem with each other to provide a continuous source of subsidized coverage for low- to middle-income individuals and families, beginning in 2014. As previously discussed, exchanges are responsible for facilitating enrollment in Medicaid.

As *originally* enacted, ACA required states to expand Medicaid to certain individuals who are under age 65 with income up to 133%[142] of the federal poverty level (FPL), beginning in 2014. This reform not only expanded eligibility to a group that generally is not eligible for Medicaid (low-income childless adults), but also raised Medicaid's mandatory income eligibility level for certain existing groups to 133% of the FPL. States were required to do this mandatory expansion as a condition of receipt of Medicaid federal financial participation. Given that premium credits would be available through all state exchanges at the same time as this Medicaid expansion, the law envisioned that all individuals with income up to 400% FPL would have access to subsidized coverage, regardless of their state of residency.

On June 28, 2012, the United States Supreme Court issued its decision in *National Federation of Independent Business v. Sebelius*. The Court held that the federal government cannot terminate current Medicaid program federal matching funds if a state refuses to expand its Medicaid program to include non-elderly, non-pregnant adults under 133% of the federal poverty level. If a state accepts the new ACA Medicaid expansion funds, it must abide by the new expansion coverage rules, but, based on the Court's opinion, it appears that a state can refuse to participate in the expansion without losing any of its current federal Medicaid matching funds. All other provisions of ACA, including the entire Health Care and Education Reconciliation Act (HCERA, P.L. 111-152), remain intact. Given that some states may choose not to expand Medicaid, there is a possibility that some individuals will not have access to either Medicaid or the premium tax credits.

Regardless of whether or not a state expands its Medicaid program, the rules for coordination and facilitating enrollment between exchange plans and Medicaid will still apply. For example, an individual exchange may decide to determine eligibility for Medicaid.[143] If a person who has applied for exchange coverage is determined eligible for Medicaid, the individual exchange must enroll the person in Medicaid and share the person's information with the state Medicaid agency.

APPENDIX A. SELECTED EXCHANGE IMPLEMENTATION DATES

Table A-1. Selected Upcoming Exchange Implementation Dates

Date	Requirement
December 14, 2012	States seeking to administer a state-based exchange must submit a declaration letter and an exchange blueprint application no later than this date to be considered for exchange approval by January 1, 2013.
December 26, 2012	States must specify a benchmark plan to serve as the reference plan for the essential health benefits (EHB) for coverage years 2014 and 2015.[a] The default benchmark option, the largest plan by enrollment in the largest product in the state's small group market, will apply in cases where a state does not voluntarily select a benchmark plan.
January 1, 2013	Each state-based exchange must be approved to operate by HHS no later than this date in order to be operational on January 1, 2014.
February 15, 2013	States seeking to have a partnership exchange effective in 2014 must submit a declaration letter and an exchange blueprint application no later than this date.
October 1, 2013	Open enrollment must begin for coverage offered through an exchange for the 2014 coverage year.
January 1, 2014	Exchanges must be established and offer coverage in every state.

Source: Table prepared by CRS based on information collected from (1) ACA (P.L. 111-148, as amended); (2) 77 Federal Register 18310; and (3) Blueprint for Approval of Affordable State-based and State Partnership Insurance Exchanges, at http://cciio.cms.gov/resources/ (3) Letter from Kathleen Sebelius to State Governors, November 9, 2012, http://www.healthcare.gov/law/resources/letters/exchange-blueprintletter.pdf and Letter from Kathleen Sebelius to Republican Governors Association, November 15, 2012.

[a] This deadline was included in the proposed rule promulgated by HHS on standards related to the EHB (77 Federal Register 70644, November 26, 2012).

APPENDIX B. RISK MITIGATION PROGRAMS UNDER ACA

Table B-1. Description of Reinsurance, Risk Corridors, and Risk-Adjustment Provisions of ACA

	Reinsurance	Risk Corridors	Risk- Adjustment
Description	Reinsurance typically is thought of as insurance for insurers. When issuing policies, an insurer faces the risk that the premiums it collects will not be sufficient to cover its expenses and generate profit. Reinsurance shifts the risk of covering high expenses from the primary insurer to a reinsurer. ACA requires all health insurance issuers and third-party administrators of group health plans to contribute to a reinsurance program administered by a nonprofit reinsurance entity.	Risk corridors refer to a mechanism that adjusts payments to health plans according to a formula based on each plan's actual, allowed expenses in relation to a target amount. If a plan's expenses exceed a certain percentage above the target, the plan's payment is increased. Likewise, if a plan's expenses exceed a certain percentage below the target, the plan's payment is decreased. Under ACA, a QHP issuer whose gains are greater than 3% of the issuer's "projections" must remit charges to HHS, while HHS must make payments to a QHP issuer that experiences losses that are greater than 3% of the issuer's "projections."	Risk adjustment refers to a mechanism that adjusts payments to health plans to take into account the risk that each plan is bearing based on its enrollee population. Plans with enrollment of less than average risk will pay an assessment to the state. States will provide payments to plans with higher than average risk.

Table B-1. (Continued)

	Reinsurance	Risk Corridors	Risk- Adjustment
Objective	Provide funding to plans that enroll highest cost individuals	Limit issuer loss (and gains)	Transfer funds from lowest risk plans to highest risk plans
Goal	Offset high-cost outliers	Protect against inaccurate rate setting	Protect against adverse selection
Who Participates	Non-grandfathered individual market plans (inside and outside of exchange) are eligible for payments	Qualified Health Plans (QHPs) in the individual and small group markets Non-grandfathered individual market plans (inside and outside of exchange) are eligible for payments (inside and outside of exchange)	Non-grandfathered individual and small group market plans (inside and outside the exchange, excluding self-insured plans)
Time Frame	Three years (2014-2016)	Three years (2014-2016)	Permanent; begins after end of benefit year 2014

Source: CRS analysis of ACA.

End Notes

[1] "Utah Health Exchange," http://www.exchange.utah.gov/about-the-exchange.

[2] "Health Connector," https://www.mahealthconnector.org/portal/site/connector.

[3] The private health insurance market is made up of three segments—the large group, small group and nongroup (individual) markets. The nongroup market refers to insurance policies offered to individuals and families buying insurance on their own. Group insurance refers to health plans offered through a plan sponsor, typically an employer.

[4] Before 2016, states will have the option to define "small employers" either as those with 100 or fewer employees or 50 or fewer employees. Beginning in 2016, small employers will be defined as those with 100 or fewer employees. Beginning in 2017, states may allow large employers to obtain coverage through an exchange (but will not be required to do so).

[5] With the exception of stand-alone dental plans that are allowed to be offered in the exchanges.

[6] For additional information about ACA's private market reforms, see CRS Report R42069, Private Health Insurance Market Reforms in the Patient Protection and Affordable Care Act (ACA), by Annie L. Mach and Bernadette Fernandez.

[7] As discussed in the "Plan Management Responsibilities" section of this report, a plan has to meet certain statutory requirements to be certified as a QHP. Certain plans offered through exchanges (e.g., stand-alone dental plans) do not necessarily meet all of the criteria to be certified as a QHP; however, the plans are required to meet some criteria and are considered

QHPs for the purpose of how the exchange interacts with the plan. For example, while a stand-alone dental plan cannot meet criteria related to benefits to qualify as a QHP (because the plan only offers dental benefits), a stand-alone dental plan is still required to meet the QHP standard to annually provide benefit and rate information to the exchange.

[8] §1312(d)(3)(B) of ACA.

[9] §1312(d)(1) of ACA.

[10] §§1311(b) and 1321(c) of ACA.

[11] 77 Federal Register 18310, March 27, 2012.

[12] §1311(b) of ACA. Instructions for submitting the Declaration Letter and the Exchange Blueprint application are available at http://cciio.cms.gov/resources/files/hie-blueprint-081312.pdf.

[13] Seventeen states and D.C. have received conditional approval to operate a state exchange: CA, CO, CT, HI, ID, KY, MD, MA, MN, NV, NM, NY, OR, RI, UT, VT, and WA. Mississippi is the only other state that submitted an application to operate a state-based exchange; HHS is withholding a decision on the state's application until state officials settle an internal dispute regarding who has the authority to act on behalf of Mississippi to establish an exchange.

[14] §1321(c) of ACA.

[15] 77 Federal Register 18310, March 27, 2012. The law also requires that the HHS Secretary creates a process whereby states that were operating exchanges before January 1, 2010, can receive assistance from federal agencies to bring their exchanges into compliance with the requirements under ACA (§1322(e) of ACA).

[16] Selected exchange implementation dates are shown in Table A-1. It should be noted that the final rule on exchange establishment (77 Federal Register 18310, March 27, 2012) provides for ways in which states can change the type of exchange established in the state. For example, if a state chooses not to establish an exchange for 2014, it still may elect to do so in the future.

[17] For a comprehensive discussion of the premium tax credits, see CRS Report R41137, Health Insurance Premium Credits in the Patient Protection and Affordable Care Act (ACA), by Bernadette Fernandez and Thomas Gabe.

[18] 77 Federal Register 18310, March 27, 2012.

[19] In responding to requests for clarification regarding what would be considered "governmental," HHS has said that it will not offer further clarification of "governmental" in deference to existing state classifications. HHS has not commented on the definition of a non-profit established by a state.

[20] §1311(f)(1) of ACA. Each state participating in the regional exchange must permit the operation of the regional exchange, and the HHS Secretary has to approve the regional exchange before it can begin operation.

[21] §1311(f)(2) of ACA. The area served by a subsidiary exchange must be at least as large as a rating area approved by the HHS Secretary for purposes described in §2701 of the Public Health Service Act (PHSA).

[22] §1311(b)(2) of ACA.

[23] 77 Federal Register 18310, March 27, 2012.

[24] §1311(f)(3) of ACA and 77 Federal Register 18310, March 27, 2012. If an exchange contracts out any function of the exchange, the exchange is responsible for ensuring that the contracted entity meets all federal requirements related to the function.

[25] 77 Federal Register 18310, March 27, 2012.

[26] Ibid.

[27] §1321(c) of ACA.

[28] The partnership model is discussed in an HHS fact sheet published September 19, 2011, available at http://www.healthcare.gov/news/factsheets/2011/09/exchanges09192011a.html. The partnership model and the federally-facilitated exchange model are both discussed in the final rule on establishment of exchanges (77 Federal Register 18310, March 27, 2012). Finally, more information is provided about federally-facilitated exchanges, including partnerships, in guidance released May 16, 2012, available at http://cciio.cms.gov/resources/files/ FFE_Guidance_FINAL_VERSION_051612.pdf.

[29] 77 Federal Register 18310, March 27, 2012.

[30] Instructions for submitting the Declaration Letter and the Exchange Blueprint application are available at http://cciio.cms.gov/resources/files/hie-blueprint-081312.pdf.

[31] Center for Consumer Information and Insurance Oversight, General Guidance on Federally-facilitated Exchanges, May 16, 2012, http://cciio.cms.gov/resources/files/FFE_Guidance_FINAL_VERSION_051612.pdf.

[32] Ibid.

[33] On January 3, 2012, HHS published guidance on partnership exchanges, available at http://cciio.cms.gov /resources/ files/partnership-guidance-01-03-2013.pdf.

[34] The framework for this section is adapted from a report co-authored by Deborah Bachrach and Patricia Boozang, titled, "Federally-Facilitated Exchanges and the Continuum of State Options," available at http://www.nasi. org/research/2011/federally-facilitated-exchanges-continuum-state-options.

[35] §§1413 and 1561 of ACA. The most recent guidance (May 2011) produced by Centers for Medicare & Medicaid Services (CMS) addressing the electronic databases is available at http://www.medicaid.gov/Medicaid-CHIP-ProgramInformation/By-Topics/Data-and-Systems/Downloads/exchangemedicaiditguidance.pdf.

[36] For more information about QHPs offered through an exchange, see the "Qualified Health Plans" section of this report.

[37] The term and definition of "insurance affordability programs" is adopted from a definition in the final rule on exchange establishment (77 Federal Register 18310, March 27, 2012).

[38] §1331 of ACA requires the HHS Secretary to create a basic health program (BHP), which is a health insurance program for low-income individuals who are not eligible for Medicaid, and is offered in lieu of eligible individuals obtaining coverage through an exchange. States have the option to implement the BHP, and therefore, exchanges will interact with BHPs in only those states that choose to implement a BHP.

[39] 77 Federal Register 18310, March 27, 2012.

[40] Ibid

[41] These provisions were included as "interim final" rather than in the final rule on exchange establishment (77 Federal Register 18310, March 27, 2012), and comments were accepted on both provisions through May 11, 2012. The preamble of the final rule indicates that further guidance on these provisions is forthcoming.

[42] The eligibility criteria for advance payment of premium tax credits and cost-sharing subsidies are the same regardless of whether an individual exchange makes the determination or HHS makes the determination.

[43] 77 Federal Register 17144, March 23, 2012.

[44] On June 28, 2012, the United States Supreme Court issued its decision in National Federation of Independent Business v. Sebelius. The Court held that the federal government cannot terminate current Medicaid program federal matching funds if a state refuses to expand its Medicaid program to include non-elderly, non-pregnant adults under 133% of the federal

poverty level. If a state accepts the new ACA Medicaid expansion funds, it must abide by the new expansion coverage rules, but, based on the Court's opinion, it appears that a state can refuse to participate in the expansion without losing any of its current federal Medicaid matching funds. This decision did not affect the ACA requirement that modified adjusted gross income (MAGI) would be the new income test for most of Medicaid's covered populations beginning in 2014. For a legal analysis of the Court's decision on Medicaid, see CRS General Distribution Memorandum, Selected Issues Related to the Effect of NFIB v. Sebelius on the Medicaid Expansion Requirements in Section 2001 of the Affordable Care Act, by Kathleen S. Swendiman and Evelyne P. Baumrucker. For a comprehensive discussion about MAGI and ACA, see CRS Report R41997, Definition of Income in ACA for Certain Medicaid Provisions and Premium Credits, coordinated by Janemarie Mulvey.

[45] Before 2016, states will have the option to define "small employers" either as those with 100 or fewer employees or 50 or fewer employees. Beginning in 2016, small employers will be defined as those with 100 or fewer employees.

[46] Beginning in 2017, a state may also allow an issuer of coverage in the large group market to offer QHPs in the large group market through an exchange. If that is the case, then a qualified employer would also include an employer in the large group market.

[47] 77 Federal Register 18310, March 27, 2012.

[48] Ibid. If a state merges its individual and small group risk pools, as is allowed under §1312(c)(3) of ACA, then the SHOP may permit an employee to enroll in any QHP (including one offered in the individual market), as long as the QHP meets certain requirements for small group market plans.

[49] This information was confirmed through correspondence with analysts from the Center for Consumer Information and Insurance Oversight (CCIIO) in September 2012.

[50] §1311(d)(4)(A) of ACA.

[51] Except that, according to §1311(e)(1)(B) of ACA, the exchange may not exclude a plan because it is a fee-for-service plan, through the imposition of price controls, or on the basis that the plan provides treatments necessary to prevent patients' deaths in circumstances the exchange determines are inappropriate or too costly.

[52] In the final regulation on entities for the accreditation of exchange plans, HHS stated that the National Committee for Quality Assurance and URAC (formerly known as the Utilization Review Accreditation Commission) would serve as accrediting entities during the first phase of the accrediting process. HHS will consider other accrediting bodies and individual states at a later time. 77 Federal Register 42662, July 20, 2012.

[53] §1311(c)(1) of ACA and 77 Federal Register 18310, March 27, 2012.

[54] §1311(e)(2) of ACA.

[55] §1311(d)(4) of ACA. In the final rule on the establishment of exchanges (77 Federal Register 18310, March 27, 2012) it is indicated that the rating system will be addressed in future rulemaking.

[56] HHS more specifically describes the consumer assistance functions of federally-facilitated exchanges, including partnerships, in guidance available at http://cciio.cms.gov/ resources/files/ FFE_Guidance_FINAL_VERSION_ 051612.pdf.

[57] The standard format an exchange is expected to use to present QHPs is required to include the uniform outline of coverage as established under §2715 of the PHSA (§1001 of ACA). For more information about the uniform outline of coverage, see CRS Report R42069, Private Health Insurance Market Reforms in the Patient Protection and Affordable Care Act (ACA), by Annie L. Mach and Bernadette Fernandez.

[58] The final rule on exchange establishment (*77* Federal Register 18310, March 27, 2012) does not specify the content or quantity of these outreach and education activities, but it does require that the activities must be accessible to all audiences, including to individuals with disabilities and those with limited English proficiency.

[59] §1311(i) of ACA and *77* Federal Register 18310, March 27, 2012.

[60] §1311(c)(4) of ACA. The survey is only for those QHPs that had more than 500 enrollees in the previous year. To date, HHS has not released any information about this survey.

[61] §1311(d)(6) of ACA.

[62] §1311(d)(7) of ACA.

[63] *77* Federal Register 18310, March 27, 2012.

[64] Ibid.

[65] §1311(d)(5) of ACA.

[66] *77* Federal Register 18310, March 27, 2012.

[67] §1313 of ACA.

[68] These criteria are included in the final rule related to the establishment of exchanges (*77* Federal Register 18310, March 27, 2012).

[69] For an overview of the rulemaking authority given to federal agencies under ACA, see CRS Report R42431, Upcoming Rules Pursuant to the Patient Protection and Affordable Care Act: Fall 2011 Unified Agenda, by Maeve P. Carey and Michelle D. Christensen.

[70] §1321(a)(1) of ACA.

[71] §1411(c) of ACA.

[72] §1311 of ACA.

[73] The CRS Congressional Distribution (CD) memorandum, "Patient Protection and Affordable Care Act: Health Insurance Exchange Planning and Establishment Grants" by C. Stephen Redhead and Annie L. Mach, includes a table that shows the federal grants (discussed in this section) that have been awarded to each state and the District of Columbia. The memorandum is available upon request from the memorandum's authors.

[74] §1311(a) of ACA. Some contend that the law does not contain explicit appropriation authority for the operation of federally-facilitated exchanges, as §1311 only says that the Secretary may award planning and establishment grants to states. However, in regard to the federally-facilitated exchange, the law does say that, "...the Secretary shall (directly or through agreement with a not-for-profit entity) establish and operate such exchange within the state and the Secretary shall take such actions as are necessary to implement such other requirements" (§1321(c)(1)(B)).

[75] All exchanges are expected to be self-sustaining by January 1, 2015. In guidance, however, HHS clarified that planning and establishment grants awarded through December 31, 2014, may be used for approved establishment activities after that date. For more information, see http://cciio.cms.gov/resources/files/ Files2/11282011/ exchange_q_and_a.pdf.pdf.

[76] Alaska is the only state that did not apply for a planning grant. Three states, Florida, Louisiana, and New Hampshire, have stated that they plan to return some or all of their planning grant funds. For more information about which states have received grants, see http://www.healthcare.gov/news/factsheets/ 2011/05/ exchanges05232011a.html.

[77] The 34 states that have received a level one grant so far are: AL, AZ, AR, CA, CO, CT, DE, HI, ID, IL, IN, IA, KY, ME, MD, MA, MI, MN, MS, MO, NE, NV, NJ, NM, NY, NC, OR, PA, RI, SD, TN, VT, WA, WV, and D.C. The states that have received level two grants, to date, are CA, CT, KY, MA, MD, NV, NY, OR, RI, VT, WA, and D.C.

[78] For more information, see CRS Congressional Distribution Memo, "Patient Protection and Affordable Care Act: Health Insurance Exchange Planning and Establishment Grants," by

Annie L. Mach and C. Stephen Redhead. The memorandum is available to congressional staff upon request from the authors.

[79] §1561 of ACA: §3021 of PHSA.

[80] The seven grantees are Kansas, Maryland, New York, Oklahoma, Oregon, Wisconsin, and a multi-state consortium led by the University of Massachusetts Medical School (which includes Connecticut, Maine, Massachusetts, Rhode Island, and Vermont). Three states, Kansas, Oklahoma, and Wisconsin, have since stated their intention to return some or all of the grant. For more information, see http://www.cbpp.org/files/ CBPP-Analysis-on-the-Status-of-StateExchange-Implementation.pdf.

[81] HealthCare.gov, "States Leading the Way on Implementation: HHS Awards "Early Innovator" Grants to Seven States," press release, February 16, 2011, http://www.healthcare.gov/news/factsheets/2011/02/ exchanges02162011a.html.

[82] Center for Consumer Information and Insurance Oversight, "Affordable Insurance Exchanges: Update and Upcoming Implementation Forums," press release, May 16, 2012, http://cciio.cms.gov/resources/factsheets/ affordable_insurance_exchanges.html.

[83] §1302(a)-(d) of ACA.

[84] This applies to all exchange enrollees whose insurance is affected by additional state benefit mandates, not just those exchange enrollees eligible for premium tax credits and cost-sharing subsidies. §1311(d)(3)(B) of ACA.

[85] See "Selected Medical Benefits: A Report from the Department of Labor to the Department of Health and Human Services," Department of Labor, April 15, 2011, http://www.bls.gov/ncs/ebs/sp/selmedbensreport.pdf.

[86] "Essential Health Benefits Bulletin," Center for Consumer Information and Insurance Oversight, December 16, 2011, p.8, http://cciio.cms.gov/resources/files/Files2/12162011/essential_health_benefits_bulletin.pdf; Department of Health and Human Services, "Patient Protection and Affordable Care Act; Standards Related to Essential Health Benefits, Actuarial Value, and Accreditation; Proposed Rule," 77 Federal Register 70644, November 26, 2012.

[87] In the final regulation on data collection to support essential health benefits standards, HHS stated that it will collect data from the insurance carriers that offer the three largest health plans (by enrollment) in the small group market within each state. The data collection is for purposes of identifying a potential "default benchmark plan" for each state. HHS intends to make publicly available the "information on the final state selections of benchmarks...as soon as possible." 77 Federal Register 42661, July 20, 2012.

[88] See "Essential Health Benefits: Comparing Benefits in Small Group Products and State and Federal Employee Plans," Office of the Assistant Secretary for Planning and Evaluation, December 2011, http://aspe.hhs.gov/health/ reports/2011/MarketComparison/rb.shtml; "Essential Health Benefits: List of the Largest Three Small Group Products by State," Center for Consumer Information and Insurance Oversight, July 3, 2012, http://cciio.cms.gov/resources/files/ largest-smgroup-products-7-2-2012.pdf.PDF; and "Frequently Asked Questions on Essential Health Benefits Bulletin," Centers for Medicare and Medicaid Services, February 17, 2012, http://cciio.cms.gov/resources/files/Files2/02172012/ ehb-faq-508.pdf.

[89] Center for Consumer Information and Insurance Oversight, Frequently Asked Questions on Essential Health Benefits Bulletin, February 17, 2012, available at http://cciio.cms.gov/resources/files/Files2/02172012/ehb-faq-508.pdf.

[90] Each state's proposed benchmark plan is available at, http://cciio.cms.gov/resources/data/ehb.html.

[91] Ibid.

[92] The cost-sharing limits that are part of the essential health benefits package mirror the limits applicable to high-deductible health plans (HDHPs) that qualify to be paired with health savings accounts (HSAs). For 2012, the cost-sharing limits for HSA-qualified HDHPs are $6,050 for single coverage, and $12,100 for family coverage. Given that the existing limits are updated annually and ACA cost-sharing requirements become effective in 2014, the cost-sharing limits in 2014 will likely be different than the 2012 levels.

[93] While actuarial value (AV) is a useful measure, it is only one component that addresses the value of any given benefit package. AV, by itself, does not address other important features of coverage, such as total (dollar) value, network adequacy, and premiums.

[94] While actuarial value is calculated based on costs for an entire population, it does not mean that every person enrolled in the same plan will have the same expenses, because in any given group some people use relatively little care while others use a great deal. Given that actuarial value reflects cost-sharing, such a measure may be useful to consumers when comparing different health plans.

[95] "Critical Issues in Health Reform: Actuarial Equivalence," American Academy of Actuaries, May 2009, p. 4, available online at http://www.actuary.org/pdf/health/equivalence_may09.pdf.

[96] "Actuarial Value and Cost-Sharing Reductions Bulletin," Center for Consumer Information and Insurance Oversight, February 24, 2012, http://cciio.cms.gov/resources/files/Files2/02242012/Av-csr-bulletin.pdf, p. 5.

[97] For more information about these plan types, see the "Multi-State Plans" and the "Consumer Operated and Oriented Plans" sections of this report.

[98] For more information about these plan types, see the "Child-Only Qualified Health Plans" and the "Catastrophic Plan" sections of this report.

[99] Plans that are offered both inside and outside of exchanges must charge the same premium. In addition, ACA allows the types of health plans that are currently offered in the private market to continue to be offered once the exchanges have been established, as long as those other plan types comply with applicable federal and state law.

[100] §1301 of ACA.

[101] §1311(c) of ACA.

[102] In guidance released December 10, 2012, HHS indicated that a state can allow an issuer that contracts with the state's Medicaid agency as a managed care organization (MCO) to offer a QHP in an exchange. The QHP would be available on a limited-enrollment basis to certain populations, and its availability would be intended to ease individuals' transitions between Medicaid or CHIP and private insurance. HHS indicated that further guidance on these "bridge" QHPs is forthcoming. For more information, see http://cciio.cms.gov/resources/files/exchanges-faqs-12-10-2012.pdf.

[103] §1301(a)(1)(C)(iii) of ACA; and 77 Federal Register 18415, March 27, 2012.

[104] §1334 of ACA.

[105] §1334(a) of ACA.

[106] OPM administers FEHBP and, among other duties, is authorized to negotiate benefit and premium levels with health plans that participate in FEHBP. For more information about OPM's role in FEHBP, see CRS Report RS21974, Federal Employees Health Benefits Program (FEHBP): Available Health Insurance Options, by Annie L. Mach.

[107] 77 Federal Register 18310, March 27, 2012. To date, OPM has not yet promulgated regulations related to MSQHPs.

[108] §1302(f) of ACA.

[109] 77 Federal Register, 18469, March 27, 2012.

[110] §1322(a)(2) of ACA.

[111] §1322 of ACA and 76 Federal Register 77392, December 13, 2011.

[112] According to the final rule on CO-OPs (76 Federal Register 77392, December 13, 2011), only two-thirds of plans offered by CO-OP loan recipients must be CO-OP QHPs offered in the individual and small group markets, indicating that CO-OP loan recipients may offer health plans that will not necessarily be available in the individual and small group markets, whether inside or outside an exchange (i.e., Medicare managed care plans).

[113] Non-profit entities in the following states have received CO-OP program loans: AZ, CO, CT, IA, IL, KY, LA, MA, MD, ME, MI, MT, NE, NJ, NM, NV, NY, OH, OR, SC, TN, UT, VT, WI. For more information, see http://www.healthcare.gov/news/factsheets/2012/02/coops02212012a.html.

[114] §644 of the American Taxpayer Relief Act of 2012.

[115] §1302(e) of ACA.

[116] Beginning in 2014, ACA requires individuals to maintain health insurance, with some exceptions. For additional information about this provision, see CRS Report R41331, Individual Mandate and Related Information Requirements under ACA, by Janemarie Mulvey and Hinda Chaikind.

[117] The deductible for exchange catastrophic plans mirror the cost-sharing limits applicable to high-deductible health plans (HDHPs) that qualify to be paired with health savings accounts (HSAs). For 2012, the cost-sharing limits for HSA-qualified HDHPs are $6,050 for single coverage, and $12,100 for family coverage. Given that the existing limits are updated annually and the exchanges become operational in 2014, the deductible for exchange catastrophic plans in 2014 will likely be different than the 2012 HDHP/HSA limits.

[118] §1001 of ACA; Section 2713 of the Public Health Service Act.

[119] §1311(d)(2)(B)(ii) of ACA.

[120] §1401 of ACA.

[121] While a premium credit recipient could choose to wait until the end of the tax year to claim the credit, as part of filing federal income taxes, the most likely scenario is for that individual to choose to receive the tax credit in the form of advanced payments, to coincide with the monthly payment of insurance premiums.

[122] §1402 of ACA.

[123] §1412(a)(3) of ACA.

[124] Household income is measured according to the current tax definition for "modified adjusted gross income" (MAGI). For a comprehensive discussion about MAGI and ACA, see CRS Report R41997, Definition of Income in ACA for Certain Medicaid Provisions and Premium Credits, coordinated by Janemarie Mulvey.

[125] An exception is made for lawfully present aliens with income below 100% of the FPL, who are ineligible for Medicaid for the first five years that they are lawfully present. These taxpayers will be treated as though their income is exactly 100% of FPL for purposes of the premium credit.

[126] The definition of minimum essential coverage is broad. It includes Medicare Part A, Medicaid, the State Children's Health Insurance Program (CHIP), Tricare, the TRICARE for Life program, the veteran's health care program, the Peace Corps program, a government plan (local, state, federal) including the Federal Employees Health Benefits Program (FEHBP) and any plan established by an Indian tribal government, any plan offered in the individual, small group or large group market, a grandfathered health plan,

and any other health benefits coverage, such as a state health benefits risk pool, as recognized by the HHS Secretary in coordination with the Treasury Secretary.

[127] ACA considers an employer-sponsored plan "unaffordable" if the employee's premium contribution to the employer's self-only plan exceeds 9.5% of household income. An employer-sponsored plan does not provide "minimum value" if it covers less than 60% of total allowed costs (on average).

[128] For a comprehensive discussion of the premium tax credits, including illustrative examples of possible credit amounts, see CRS Report R41137, Health Insurance Premium Credits in the Patient Protection and Affordable Care Act (ACA), by Bernadette Fernandez and Thomas Gabe.

[129] See the "Eligibility for Premium Tax Credits and Cost-Sharing Subsidies" section in this report for more information.

[130] This proposed approach for implementing the cost-sharing subsidies was discussed in a bulletin issued by HHS: "Actuarial Value and Cost-Sharing Reductions Bulletin," February 24, 2012, - http://cciio.cms.gov/ resources/files/ Files2/02242012/Av-csr-bulletin.pdf.

[131] See previous discussion of precious metal designations for exchange plans under the section "Levels of Plan Generosity" in this report.

[132] The cost-sharing limits that are part of the essential health benefits package mirror the limits applicable to high-deductible health plans (HDHPs) that qualify to be paired with health savings accounts (HSAs). For 2012, the cost-sharing limits for HSA-qualified HDHPs are $6,050 for single coverage, and $12,100 for family coverage. Given that the existing limits are updated annually and ACA cost-sharing requirements become effective in 2014, the cost-sharing limits in 2014 will likely be different than the 2012 levels.

[133] For additional information about the cost-sharing subsidies, including illustrative examples, see CRS Report R41137, Health Insurance Premium Credits in the Patient Protection and Affordable Care Act (ACA), by Bernadette Fernandez and Thomas Gabe.

[134] See the "Eligibility for Premium Tax Credits and Cost-Sharing Subsidies" section in this report for more information.

[135] The constitutionality of the individual mandate has been the centerpiece of numerous legal challenges to ACA. In March of 2012, the United States Supreme Court heard arguments related to the constitutionality question, along with other legal issues. On June 28, 2012, the Court issued its decision in National Federation of Independent Business v. Sebelius, finding that the individual mandate in §5000A of the Internal Revenue Code (as added by §1501 of the Patient Protection and Affordable Care Act (ACA)), is a constitutional exercise of Congress's authority to levy taxes. For additional discussion about the Court's decision, the individual mandate, and other ACA issues, see the CRS Legal Sidebar posts under "Health and Medicine," http://www. crs.gov/analysis/legalsidebar/pages/ default.aspx?source= legalSidebar.

[136] For a list of the types of coverage that qualify as "minimum essential coverage" and additional information about the individual mandate see CRS Report R41331, Individual Mandate and Related Information Requirements under ACA, by Janemarie Mulvey and Hinda Chaikind.

[137] In the final rule on exchange establishment (77 Federal Register 18310, March 27, 2012), HHS indicated that in future rulemaking it will address the process exchanges will use to provide certificates of exemption.

[138] For additional information about employer requirements under ACA, see CRS Report R41159, Summary of Potential Employer Penalties Under the Patient Protection and Affordable Care Act (PPACA), by Janemarie Mulvey.

[139] §1401(a) of ACA; adding a new §36B(c)(2)(C) to the Internal Revenue Code.

[140] For additional information about ACA's private market reforms, see CRS Report R42069, Private Health Insurance Market Reforms in the Patient Protection and Affordable Care Act (ACA), by Annie L. Mach and Bernadette Fernandez.

[141] Note that ACA does not prohibit such carriers from offering coverage outside of exchanges – see §1312 (d)(1)(A) of ACA.

[142] In addition, there is a 5% income disregard, so that the effective limit is 138% of the FPL.

[143] For more information about Medicaid, see the "Eligibility for Medicaid and CHIP" section of this report.

INDEX

A

B

C

D

E

F

G

T

U

V

W